TEARS OF A *Suffering* SOUL

Jeannette Roberson

Copyright © 2020 by Jeannette Roberson

All rights reserved. No part of this publication may be reproduced, distributed, or transmitted in any form or by any means, including photocopying, recording, or other electronic or mechanical methods, without the prior written permission of the publisher, except in the case of brief quotations embodied in critical reviews and certain other noncommercial uses permitted by copyright law. For permission requests, write to the publisher, addressed "Attention: Permissions Coordinator," at the address below.

ISBN: 978-1-7346343-9-6

Publishing By:
DemiCo National, LLC
3001 9th Avenue, SW
Huntsville, Alabama 35805

DEDICATIONS

I dedicate this book to those who shaped my life with grace, faith, and unconditional love.

My wonderful and loving children

My Mother and Sweet Angel,
Ciller Jean Nalls
January 16, 1958-September 30, 2010

All 4 of my Grandparents
who loved me without restraint

Alonzo Nalls,
a Man of Courage, Strength, and Integrity

Bobby Goodloe,
An Honorable and Loving man that played
a major role in my life. The man I still call "Dad"

TABLE OF CONTENTS

INTRODUCTION	9
1. NETTIE POOH	11
2. THE BOOGIE MAN	22
3. I DO…I DID	32
4. SLEEPING WITH DANGER	42
5. LAUGHABLE LOVE	53
6. THE NEW NORM	61
7. THE SUFFRAGE	78
8. THE TRUTH OF MY TEARS	97

INTRODUCTION

Rape, sex, love, and intimacy; I became confused about these terms at an incredibly young age. My body hasn't been my own since I was fourteen years old. When I was a little girl, I believed in the Easter Bunny, Tooth Fairy and even Santa. Yet, it wasn't until I met the real Boogie Man that I believed in him too. I was first told that girls mature faster than boys before I started my menstrual cycle. Would this help me understand the transformation from boys to men? Would this help me understand my transformation from being a girl into womanhood?

My views on maturity and womanhood were screwed up from the beginning. Even when I didn't know what it meant to be mature, I felt as if it was something honorable that girls should be happy to become while boys were not required to do so. It sure as hell didn't help that the moment, I got my period, and I barely knew what to expect. Maybe I didn't work as hard as the grown-up women in my family, but I did housework and helped take care of my cousins as if I was a Mom also. It was almost inevitable that I would crave womanhood before girlhood was over. Is it because womanhood is marketed towards little girls in ways that manhood is never marketed to little boys?

While responsibility is at times taught as an option to boys, it becomes a duty to girls that we must wear on our backs at an early age. When we tell girls that they mature faster than boys, we put the responsibility of patience on their shoulders when many times maturity isn't the boy's issue. Sometimes the boy is just evil, selfish, manipulative, and toxic. We women get tired of having to go through life pardoning boys and their poor behaviors simply under the idea that it is just taking him longer to mature.

Women are always expected to have reached and developed the best version of themselves before getting married. We were taught to care for others long before we were taught to care for ourselves. The idea that taking care of others is self-care was deposited into our femininity at a young age. So, I did what I believed I was supposed to do. I was patient with the boys. When they ignored me, I was patient. When they broke my heart, I was patient. When they raped me, left me, impregnated me and even when they beat me, I was patient with the boys.

As I began to mature, I found myself becoming toxic in many areas. Maybe it was because of the shame and guilt that I felt as my innocence was taken away from me at an early age. As I dealt with patience repeatedly, I began feeling lost, hurt, and feeling alone. Was I insane for doing the same things over and over expecting different results?

So, how is it that boys turn into the Boogie Men themselves? How do young girls become a target? Is it because we are reared in broken homes, where there is no father or positive male role models present? Could it even be because there were mothers like myself who reared her children with a tainted heart and a broken soul?

I have suffered for many years, and now my healing process has begun. Now, I am ready as I share the tears of my suffering soul.

CHAPTER ONE

Nettie Pooh

"Jeannette?", Her voice echoed from inside the house.

"Ma'am?" I asked throwing my leg over the bicycle that was much too tall for me to ride, but it was the only bicycle that I had. In fact, my cousins and I shared bicycles as we did most things during my childhood. I balanced myself on the bike that I had only recently learned was a boy's bike, as I looked to the porch. Within a moment, her silhouette emerged from the screen door. She did not open the door. Instead, she dried her hands on the only apron I had ever seen tied around her waist. She spoke.

"Where you going? Your mama is working this evening, and you don't need to stray too far. You're going to bible study with me tonight." She said. "I'm not gonna chase you down to find you when it's time to go."

"I'm just going to Mary 'nem house." I explained hoping she would grant my wish. I could hear the children's voices echoing down the street as they played. The sound seemed to be calling me.

"They need to be getting ready to go to somebody's church too." She said.

"They are going to somebody's church. Mary said they were." I don't know what made me lie so foolishly and easily, but I didn't want to go to church with my grandmother that night any more than I did any other night. Mary and her family drove to church. Just like everywhere else she went, my grandmother walked to church. She never learned to drive. She was a proud woman, and she would rarely accept rides to the market, church, or courthouse when she had to tend to business. I hated the long walks, but there I was always walking alongside her. She just walked and moaned and walked and sang.

"Mama, let the girl go on and play. She's a child." Uncle Ken said walking down the street. He spoke to her, but he smiled at me. I smiled back. I loved this man. He entered the yard and made his way to the porch.

"You calling the shots at my house?", Grandma asked him.

"No, ma'am. She got her coat and hat and I'm just saying that she's gonna do what she knows you expect her to do. Ain't that right, Nettie Pooh?" He said turning back to look at me. I nodded, zipping my coat up to my neck. Damn, lying felt good. I knew damn well that I didn't have any intentions of coming back in time for the walk to church, but to keep the black on my back I knew I had to at least make an effort to do the right thing. I knew that just as soon as I got free from her site that coat was hitting the ground. It was bulky, and I bout killed myself once before trying to race on my bicycle while wearing that giant coat.

"I ain't going nowhere, but down the street", I said. I became frustrated. It was not too often that I got to experience moments of just being a kid without the responsibility of supervising or babysitting my many younger cousins. Well, on this day it was just me, and I wanted to enjoy my own friends. I watched Uncle Ken stare at Grandma. His smile faded. She was silent. He saw the same thing that I saw. While

I did not understand what the expression draped across her stern face meant, I knew that something was not right.

"Mama, what is it?", He asked, opening the screen door for a better look at her.

She pulled the door closed from him. He looked at her as I watched. By this time, I was certain that I would not get the few hours of play with Mary before church, so I removed myself from the bike.

"You want her to be able to play, then you stay out here on this porch and watch her", She said.

"Mama, I got stuff to do."

"You stay out here, and you don't take your eyes from her. Do you hear me?" She said, raising her voice. He nodded, removed his cap, and made his way to a chair on the porch. Grandma disappeared into the house.

"Go head, Nettie Pooh. Go play with your friends." He said as Mary and the other kids started down the street towards me on their much nicer bicycles.

"You coming?" Mary shouted to me as she zoomed by me. Something inside of me would not let me get back on the bicycle. Something was wrong, and my Grandmother knew it. I knew it. My grandmother was a very spiritual woman, and she loved God in a way that I did not and could not understand at such a young age. God often gave her feelings, intuitions, and discernment of when matters where off with her children and grandchildren. She worked hard to maintain such an intimate relationship with God. I had seen that look on her face before, and she was scared. You must understand that my grandmother was the strongest woman that I had ever known, so for her to be afraid, made me afraid.

"I ain't going." I said to Mary. "I got stuff to do." Mary and the kids did not respond as they turned the corner and quickly vanished. I pushed the bike into the yard and left it near the porch.

"Why you ain't going to play with your friends?", Uncle Ken asked.

"What's wrong with Grandma?"

"Don't worry about Mama. She's alright. She just worries about all of us too much sometimes. It ain't nothing for you to be worried about. I'm gonna always take care of you." He said. I didn't know how to respond to him. He wasn't my father. I rarely saw or spoke to my father. So, whether it was Uncle Ken or one of my Mama's boyfriends, I didn't know how to respond to a man saying things I thought my Daddy should only say to me.

I made my way into the small house. I could hear her whimpers and prayers, so I stood still in the living room. I did not want to make a sound. I stared at the photos of my grandmother, and our family. We all looked so happy.

My mother and I stayed with my grandmother for most of my childhood. My grandmother was a beautiful woman. Her skin was a dark caramel color and she had black silky hair. She was a prestigious lady with honor. My Grandmother was respected everywhere as a true woman of God and faithfulness.

Was she perfect? No, but who is? However, she was perfect in the eyes of those who loved her. She only drank one beer in her whole life. In retrospect, the home that always seemed so large as a child, was not large at all. My grandmother's small home consisted of two bedrooms, and one bathroom. More than one generation of our family lived in the home, sometimes all at once. Throughout her years of working, she found time to raise children, do housework, go to church, and teach all of us about love and life. Even though she was loving, she was tough, and this was the type of tough that could only come from a southern black woman who had survived Jim Crow laws and segregation.

We would get whippings with switches if we had arguments among ourselves. She would tell us to make up by hugging each other. For some reason I was always the one that had the biggest problem doing this. I soon came to realize that hugging was a form of love and communication. Even though I was an only child, I had several cousins that needed my love and my attention. Being the oldest cousin, I had the most responsibilities. During the warm months, I would hang wet clothes outside on the clothesline. There was an apple tree and a peach tree in the back yard that we would pick from. Polk salad grew there also, and I would often gather some as part of our meals.

At times, I would have to stand in line for free food, such as peanut butter and cheese. There were neighbors, and specific family members who would send money or bring food to help during these difficult times. I never understood how our food supply would sometimes run low, but we always seemed to have plenty during Thanksgiving and Christmas. The women in my family were the best of cooks, and everything was always made from scratch. We had chicken and dressing, sweet potato pies, chocolate cake, ham, beans, and rolls; just to name a few of the items that sat on the kitchen table. There was always a nice clean and crisp tablecloth with decorative bowls and other dishes on the dining room table. Throughout everything, my grandmother always made us feel loved and safe. So, why would I ever believe such evil could exist in the world I knew at that age? She would pray every night before she went to bed and every morning when she awoke. There were times that we did not have utilities. If we became hot, she would stay awake all night and fan us with newspaper. I was always afraid of the dark. For light, we used candles and the glares from the streetlights.

"Amen". I heard her say. The prayer was over. She entered the kitchen. By this time, I had grabbed a bowl of corn to shuck and sat at the kitchen table.

"You wash your hands Nettie Pooh?", She asked, returning to the stove.

"Yes, Ma'am."

"Why you ain't out there with your friends?"

"I don't know. I ain't feel like it", I said. She continued stirring in the large pot.

That night the Klan marched in front of our home. Policemen on horses accompanied them. I was frightened. The neighbors were all quiet. I had never seen such a site, but I knew what I was looking at. I knew that this was the evil that had plagued my Grandmother's spirit. This made me want to be even closer to her. I could not nestle myself beneath her enough.

After a while, the march ended, and I was sent into the backyard as a few of the church members and neighbors joined in my Grandmother's living room.

I sat on the back doorstep so I could hear what was happening.

"It's intimidation." I heard Deacon Jones say. I recognized his voice as the voice of the man who prayed much too long about the same things every Sunday.

"Well, is it working on y'all? Are y'all intimidated? I ain't." I heard my grandmother say.

"Sister, we're not intimidated but we are just being realistic." Another woman explained.

"I'm being faithful", Grandma said.

"We're all being faithful, but white folks ain't happy about President Reagan giving us Dr. King Day tomorrow. They trying to scare us off from marching", Deacon Jones said.

"It's been fifteen years since they killed Dr. King. It took them fifteen years to do right by him, and me and mine ain't gonna be scared off. We're going down to that courthouse tomorrow and we're marching for Dr. King. If y'all ain't going with us, then fine." Grandma explained. A short while later the home emptied. We didn't make it to church that night. I was relieved. I did not want to walk to church. By the time I got in bed that night, Mama made it home. She was exhausted and it was obvious.

The next morning, we did exactly as my Grandma had planned. We dressed in warm clothes, and we walked to the county courthouse to join the other blacks to celebrate and march in honor of Dr. King.

Every part of my body seemed to be warm but my feet. They were freezing and ached as we marched and marched. Many of the faces I recognized from the community or church. They sang songs I had never heard outside of the church or my grandmother's home. I was quiet, but I marched as well. She held my hand tight as we passed by the policemen sitting on their tall horses. I made eye contact with the horse, then the officer. He seemed to almost look through me. I looked ahead as my grandmother continued singing, *We're Marching on To Zion.*

    I adored growing up in my grandmother's home. After a while, I no longer resented our long walks, talks, or church goings. I felt something being deposited into my young soul that I clearly knew that I needed. I was baptized when I was about 11 years old. Before I was baptized, the preacher spoke with me. He stated that for me to be saved I must hear the word, believe the word, and repent for my sins. I had to confess my faith, be baptized, and remain faithful. I felt as if I understood this completely and was ready to enter a new world with God. I wondered if God could speak to me the way He spoke to my Grandmother. I went to Sunday school every week, as well as all other church services, and was obedient to God. So, I believed I was ready to begin my journey.

    I was maturing fast. I now cooked, cleaned, and cared for the younger children as I neared my teens. I felt mature, responsible, and almost like a woman. However, I still longed for contact with my father. I loved Uncle ken, and I know that he loved me, but he was not my Dad.

On a particular afternoon, I sat in the kitchen helping Grandma shuck corn again. Mama entered the house. She went to the sink and washed her hands. Grandma didn't speak. Mama joined us at the table.

"You alright, baby?" Grandma asked her.

"Yea Mama. I'm just tired, but it's finally paying off." Mama said.

"Well, baby, if you be faithful over a few things the Lord will make you ruler over many." Mama nodded, hesitated, and then spoke.

"Ma, I got a new job and it's a good job. I mean it is much better than these little jobs I've been had around here." Mama said.

"That's good! I'm happy for you, Baby."

"It's in Decatur." Mama blurted. The room was silent. I looked at Grandma. She reached beneath the table to wipe her hands on her apron.

"Nettie Pooh, go to your room. Let me talk to your Mama." I did as told. Grandma did not compromise on refusing to allow children to hear adult conversations. I went to the small bedroom and wondered of Decatur. I had never heard of Decatur and I had no idea of how near or far this town could be. I wondered if Mama would let me stay with Grandma. I sat on the bed. A few moments later, the phone rang. Mama and Grandma were deep into their discussion and apparently did not hear the ringing phone, so I made my way to Grandma's room and answered the phone.

"Hello?"

"Hey, Nette. That you?" Antonio asked. Damn, I was glad I answered the phone before Mama or Grandma answered.

"Yea. It's me. You better be glad my Grandma didn't answer the phone."

"You don't want me to call you?" He asked in the cutest and most innocent voice.

"I don't know. Yea I guess so." I said sitting on Grandma's bed. There was a silence. I was 13 and had absolutely no idea of what I should say next.

"I like you Nette." He said. "You like me too, right?"

"I think so."

"You think? Either you do or you don't.", He laughed.

"I do," I blushed.

"Cool," He said. I didn't know what we should say next, but I spoke.

"Antonio, do you know where Decatur is?"

"Yea. It ain't too far from here. It's like an hour drive. Why?" He asked.

"I think we're moving," I said.

"Are you serious? How are you gonna be my girlfriend if you are in Decatur?" He asked.

"Girlfriend?" I laughed. I ended the conversation as I heard Grandma's chair slide across the kitchen floor. Sure enough, we moved to Decatur. The adjustment was not as bad as I had assumed. Decatur was slightly larger than Sheffield, and I knew how to make friends. So, I would make this work. I still had my phone calls with Grandma, Mary, and Antonio. I was making friends across our apartment complex also, so this could work. I felt relieved to not have to be the caretaker for my younger cousins anymore. Decatur started to look promising. I even loved having my own bedroom. My bedroom consisted of white iron twin beds, with the gold balls and pink matching comforters. For the first time in my life I felt like a little princess, and it felt amazing.

I can still remember the first night Richard put his hand between my legs. He left my bedroom with an erection, shut the door behind him, and returned to my mother's bed to make love to her with the same hands he had just used to kill Nettie Pooh. I covered my ears with the pillows. I felt myself drowning in my own tears as the phone rang. The phone continued ringing, and it had to be Antonio. I needed to hear his voice. I needed to tell him what had just occurred. I was terrified to leave the room. What if Richard caught me in the hall? I trembled and struggled to catch my breath. Could I make it to the kitchen to answer the ringing phone? I jumped from the bed and dashed from the room. I could hear the sounds of Richard on top of my mother. I snatched the phone from the wall as I gasped for air.

"HELLO?", I said.

"Nettie Pooh?" Grandma's voice said. "Something doesn't seem right, Nettie. Everything okay?". I struggled to catch my breath as I heard the door opening from Mama's bedroom.

CHAPTER TWO

The Boogie Man

Who would have thought that Nettie Pooh would die at fourteen years old? Certainly, I never thought of such a thing, but she did. I did. I died when I was fourteen years old and I knew it. I felt it when it happened. I felt my soul leave my body the moment the man that had sex with my mother every night put his hand in between my legs and gripped my vagina like a toy that belonged to him.

The child that was spoken of so highly in Sunday school, and before the congregation had died and no amount of love could ever revive what had been taken from her. Would anyone one day march for her as they did Dr. King? She too had been assassinated and she would continue being assassinated repeatedly night after night. Would anyone give a damn about the innocence, virtue, and faith that had been stripped from this child who had no greater dreams than to love.

You must understand this before we go any further. My mother loved her some Richard. She was in love in a way that I never knew could exist. How could I take that from her? I adored her. How was I supposed to tell her that the man she spoke of as almost a king, spent his nights while she was working trying to rape her daughter. Why in the hell did I need to tell her? Why couldn't she see it for herself? I could not answer all the questions in my mind, and I could not bring myself to expose Richard as the monster that truly he was. So, I became angry. This was a type of anger that I knew would lead to disaster, but dammit; I did not care. I needed relief. I needed a break. I needed to feel as if I had some sort of say so or control over my dismantling teenage life. I began to sleep fully dressed in sweatshirts, pants, and even my tennis shoes. I would push the other bed or dresser onto the door to avoid Richard entering my room at night. He was unstoppable. He was evil. I could not sleep, for peace was no longer a possibility for me. During the many hours of lying awake fearing Richard, my mind began to drift to my real father. Where was he? How could he not be here? If my father was with my mother this would not be happening. We wouldn't be in Decatur. Here my Mama was breaking her back just to make ends meet and attaching herself with the Boogieman himself for any shred of assistance and my Dad was nowhere to be found. I was angry.

In my anger, I had to find a way to make sense of what my life had become. Richard had not succeeded with forcing his penis in me yet, while I knew that he was strong enough to overpower me. Perhaps, I grew to believe that he enjoyed the chase or pursuit of me. So maybe this wasn't molestation or rape at all I told myself. Maybe I did not have to completely devastate my mother. Yes, I can tolerate this. My entire life I had seen strong black women tolerate things they should have never had to tolerate, but they did what they had to do to keep surviving. I believed that I was just as strong as the other women in my family, and if this was my cross to bear, then so be it. He's just trying, but he's not going to actually rape me so it's not worth mentioning.

By the time I was fifteen, I knew that Richard would not stop until he had my virginity. I refused to let him do that to me. I wanted Antonio, even though we rarely saw one another because he was back home. I found myself pulling from Antonio. Perhaps I pulled from Antonio because I knew of his relationship with my cousin, or maybe because I felt as if he was just as much of a kid as I was. He could not save me, my father wouldn't save me, and neither could Uncle Ken. So, when the attractive Quincy showed up in the apartment complex, I knew my chance of emancipation had come. Quincy was in his early twenties, but I had never been so attracted to a man before. He smiled a lot, and his niece Nikki jumped at the opportunity to introduce us. She knew I wanted him. He knew that I wanted him from the first moment we met. I knew he would take my virginity. It did not take me long to fall in love with Quincy. We had sex.

At first, I was incredibly nervous. Quincy was older, and I could tell by the things that he did to my body, that he was experienced with many other women. I didn't want to seem as if I was just some kid, so I hoped and aimed to please him in every way that I thought would make me appear to be just as mature.

I felt sinful right after. I could almost hear my grandmother's voice in my head. I wondered if God would expose my relationship with Quincy to my grandmother as he had many other things throughout my life. I also wondered why God had not shown my grandmother that Richard was attacking me. There were so many fucking questions in my head at this time that I just needed it all to stop. I mean, when I woke up, there was something to question. I had no peace. I questioned everything because nothing made sense to me. I loved Quincy, but he refused to be seen around the complex with me. No matter how much of a woman I told myself that I was by this time, the fact is I was still legally a child and Quincy could go to prison if anyone knew that we were having sex.

Richard would stare at me as I stared at Quincy. I knew that he knew I cared for Quincy. Perhaps seeing another man care for me frightened him. Perhaps he feared I would expose his attempts to rape me to Quincy. I had no intentions of doing so, I just wanted the life I believed that Quincy and I would have together. This was the life that Quincy promised we would have together. I found myself avoiding Antonio as we drifted further and further apart. I found peace within my moments of lying beneath Quincy. I struggled to remove my clothes and be fully naked before him. I became angry that my mother's boyfriend had taken my ability to fully give myself to another man.

"I love you." I said as he rested on top of me. His shoulder practically covered my mouth, so I wasn't sure if he heard me. "I love you, Quincy". I repeated.

"I heard you the first time." He said, pulling himself out of me and sitting of the side of the bed. I glanced at the unopened condom on the nightstand next to his bed.

"You not gonna say it back to me?" I asked almost with a bit of laughter. This was important to me, and not at all funny. However, I felt as if it was easier to act as if I were joking than to tell him that I needed his love. He never replied. I refused to believe that his silence was an indication that he did not love me. Some people just struggle to say those words, I told myself. That's it. He loves me. He's just having a hard time telling me.

"Get dressed. It's getting late." He said standing. He pulled up his sweatpants and tossed my panties to me. The panties flew above my head and landed on the floor on the other side of the bed. I stared at them on the floor. I felt different now, but I could not quite understand what I felt. I did understand that I did not like that feeling. It was a familiar feeling. For the first time, I felt used. I felt like trash. I didn't want to pick up my panties from the floor. I felt as if that would degrade me even more. He tossed my panties to me, and I did not like that. I thought of Richard.

"Whatcha doing? Hurry up." He said looking at me. I glanced at Quincy, and then back to the panties. I exhaled and picked them up. I stood to dress. I froze as I realized I had not had my period in some time. Again, I looked at the unused condom on the nightstand.

"Quincy, what time does John's market close?"

"I don't know. Ten, I think. Why?"

"What time is it now?" I asked looking around.

"You got time to make it if you run." He said tying his shoes. I looked at him. He reached for his car keys from on top of the old box television. I nodded. I kissed him and walked away. I walked from the apartment, and down the stairs. I looked towards my apartment. Sure enough, I could see Richard's silhouette in the window. I pulled my hood over my head. I started for John's Market as my ankles ached.

I began to reminisce of walking with my grandmother. I found myself even humming some of her favorite songs. They were needed in that moment, because if my newest fear was about to come true, then only the love of God could get me through it. I walked through the parking lot and pushed the door. The bell above the door chimed, and I entered. I made my way around the small convenience store first to be certain that there were no other residents of our complex in the store. I felt the old white man at the register watching me. Before long, he showed up on every aisle with me. I felt as if I was being watched.

"Can I help you find someone?"

"No sir. I'm good." I said.

"Well, hurry it up. I'm shutting down soon." He said. I nodded.

After intentionally walking past the personal care items a dozen times, my feet finally stopped before the one pregnancy test left in the store. I really hated the idea of only placing a pregnancy test on the counter before the cashier. I had planned to ease the test on the counter with a few bags of chips and maybe a soda, but the test was much more expensive than I thought. I returned the snacks and grabbed the pregnancy test. Trying to imagine what confidence looked like, I attempted to hold my head high as I placed the test before John. Maybe he would think I was a grown woman.

He avoided looking at me, instead he just shook his head as I placed the money in his hand.

"Can I Get a paper bag?", I asked.

"I only have plastic", He replied. I took the test and left the market.

With every step towards home, I felt increasingly confident that I was pregnant. I took deep breaths. I finally made it home.

"Here she is", Richard said as I entered the apartment." Mama rushed into the living room as I closed the door. I held the pregnancy test beneath my jacket.

"Jeannette, where have you been? It's late." She asked, quickly walking to me.

"I was…"

"Before you lie and say you were at Nikki's apartment, just know that I was just over there." She said. There was a silence. I glanced at Richard. He lowered the beer from his mouth.

"I walked to John's market to get a drink and chips."

"I don't see any drink or chips. Is this what you usually do when I'm at work?" Mama responded quickly. I felt as if I would cry. I felt as if I would faint. I placed my hand on the back of a nearby chair. Richard stared at me.

"Baby, cool it. Leave the girl alone. She probably just finished the snacks on the walk home. Now that I think of it, she did ask me if she could walk to the market." Richard lied. He stood and made his way to Mama. She turned to him.

"You told her that she could walk across town in this dark by herself at this hour?"

"Across town? Babe, John's Market isn't even half a mile away. You're making a big deal out of nothing."

"Don't tell me that I'm making a big deal over nothing. She is my baby, and it's not safe for her out there." She shouted. He nodded.

"We ain't got nobody else in Decatur. People are doing any and everything out there these days, and that ain't gonna happen to my child."

"It's my fault. It's my fault", He said sitting his beer on the coffee table and pulling her to him. "You have me."

"Nette, go on to your room." She said. I did as told. "Richard, you got to do better than that. That is my child, and I need you to look out for her as if she's your own."

"Don't you think that's what I'm doing?" I heard him say as I closed the bathroom door behind me. I sat the test before me on the sink.

Ten minutes later, I began to think of names of my child. I stuffed the test back into the box and made my way to my bedroom. I held a pillow over my mouth to avoid my mother hearing my tears. I felt horrible.

I waited and waited for the sound of Quincy's car and its blasting music to return to the complex. A few moments later I heard the front door close. I couldn't think of anything other than a life as a mother. How could I carry this child? I heard hip hop music in the distance, and I looked from the window for Quincy's car. Sure enough, his car entered the parking lot. I watched as my mother opened the door to her car. She worked so hard, and I appreciated her. There was no way that I could ever be the type of mother that she was. She was strong and unyielding. I was a child, and no matter how much I told myself that I was a woman when I was lying beneath Quincy, the truth is that I was a girl. I dried the tears of my suffering soul from my face.

There, in the parking lot drove the two people I needed most. How would I tell either of them that I was now pregnant? I exhaled as I realized I was sitting on the bed that usually serves as a barricade on my bedroom door. I looked out of the window as Mama's car disappeared down the street. I turned to my bedroom door.

Stricken with fear and grief, I forgot to lock and barricade the door. I jumped across the bed and dashed for the door. I felt dizzy and stumbled. I reached for the bed post. Realizing I would not make it to the door, I gasped for air as Richard entered.

"GET OUT!" I screamed as I held my stomach. He closed the door behind him and locked it. Help me God, I thought as the room began to spin. He smiled as I struggled to stand.

"You know I saved you from getting your ass beat, don't you?"

"Leave me alone!" I shouted. "Leave me alone!"

"You giving pussy to that lil' punk ass boy, and he ain't doing shit for you and your Mama!" He screamed back at me. I wanted to scream for Quincy to save me, but my fingers, face, and limbs tingled. "Here I am taking care of y'all, and you fighting me?" He raged as he tossed me further onto the bed. I immediately wrapped my arms around my stomach. It was not a thought; it was a reflex. Only a matter of minutes ago had I learned that I was pregnant, and motherhood had already birthed from my spirit. I had to protect my child. I knew that I could not fight with my hands and protect my abdomen at the same time. He climbed on top of me. I decided to not fight. I could not allow him to hurt my child. I refused to allow him to hurt my baby. I relaxed my body. I smelled his horrible breath on my neck as he kissed me. I calmed, my tears dried, and I froze as I heard the unzipping of his pants. He pulled my pants down, surprised that I no longer had any fight left. He stared into my eyes with excitement and shock, and then his smile began to fade. We locked eyes. I felt his erection leaving, as did my soul. He thrusted his hip against me one final time, but still; I did not respond or fight. Richard pulled from me. He looked at my trembling hands on my abdomen. He began to shake his head. He returned his penis to his pants and walked away. My mother's monster punched the wall as he closed the door behind him.

CHAPTER THREE

I Do…I Did

Fast. That's what southern black religious people during the early 90's called young girls who became pregnant out of wedlock. Maybe I was fast. You must understand that from the moment I first allowed a man to enter my body, something in me felt alive in a way that I had never known before. Within no time, I found myself not only having sex with Quincy, but several other young men as well. No matter who else I slept with, no one could compare to Quincy.

He wasn't just some random guy, he was Quincy. I loved him, so I gave myself to the man that I loved in the only way that I knew a woman could give herself to a man she loved. What was so wrong with that? Granted, I was fifteen, and he was in his early twenties. Granted, I lied to my mother. Granted, I lied to my boyfriend Antonio who still lived back home although he had dumped my cousin to be with me. While Quincy was not the only man or boy that I had slept with, I knew that he was the true father of my child. So, when the eight month of my pregnancy came around, and I could no longer avoid paternity questions, I had to finally tell my family something.

By this time, I had left Decatur and returned to Sheffield to live with my Aunt Tasha. I adored her. She was strong, incredibly giving, and seeing a mother such as her made me feel inspired. She was passionate about raising her children with love, honor, and respect. I did not feel judged by her, and I did not have to see the disappointment on my mother or grandmother's face every day. That was too much to bear, and the idea that Quincy no longer wanted anything to do with me was enough pressure. I couldn't handle much more. I was being asked of my plans to support a child, and I was not even old enough to get a job.

"Track meet? Girl, that's done. You're gonna have to focus on that baby now." Everyone seemed to remind me whenever I spoke of anything that meant something to me. I was willing to sacrifice whatever was needed to secure a healthy and stable future for my daughter, but I had no idea what all was needed, and my mother and grandmother were clearly too devastated to accurately explain it to me. I did not feel as if I had destroyed my life. To be honest, at that time I did not have many aspirations for my own young life. So, while I never planned on having a child at such a young age, I did not anticipate the new predicament altering my plans too much. However, the adults around me regularly reminded me of how my actions had changed their lives and subjected them to stress, ridicule, embarrassment, and more than they had never bargained for.

Telling my mother was one of the scariest conversations that I ever had with her. Of course, she talked to me about sex and boys, trying to keep me covered from sin. I chose to go out on my own and disobey her wishes. My Aunt Tasha loved me and cared for me as if I was her own child so when she finally made me face the truth, I could no longer run. I informed her that the father of my child was much older, and that he feared going to prison if I had exposed him. I knew that she was angry. She struggled to understand how I could have changed so much within such a small period of living in Decatur. I knew that I had to tell her everything. She deserved everything. She deserved my truth. A few days later, she knocked on my bedroom door.

"Nette, your Mama is in the living room. She wants to see you." She said. I hesitated as I stared out the window. I watched as the other neighborhood girls walked up and down the streets with their flat bellies, and small ankles. Their hair was straightened and silky. My hair was pulled back in a ponytail because I hated the heat of my hair on my neck. I hated that my body was always hot, and the record-breaking Alabama heat was driving me insane. "You hear me, baby?" She repeated.

"Yes, Ma'am." I said. I had not seen my mother in a while, and I was gaining weight by the minute. Although she knew I was pregnant, I was afraid for her to see me. I walked from the bedroom into the living room. She sat on the sofa. I held my stomach as she looked up at me. She gave a huge exhale. I felt my mother's heart break, and I knew that we both were fighting our tears. She felt as if she failed me, and I felt worse. I felt as if I failed her as well. In retrospect, I never felt as if I failed myself. My agony was specific. I hated that I was no longer everyone's Nettie Pooh. I was a woman now, and I did not like it as much as I thought I would.

"How are you feeling, baby?"

"I'm okay." I lied. I hated the idea of anyone expressing concern towards me, while also crying because no one expressed concern towards me. She nodded. There was an uncomfortable pause.

I hated awkward small talk, so I spoke. "I've been thinking of names. I got a whole list I've been making somewhere around here." I said as I began to look around the room. "It's not as easy as I thought it would be coming up with names. I think I have been…"

"Is that Richard's baby?" She interrupted. I froze. The room was more silent than ever before. In fact, the entire world seemed to silence at that moment. I couldn't look at her.

"I must have left the list of names in my locker."

"Marietta Jeannette Roberson! Answer me!" She shouted. I shivered and looked at her. She took a breath and lowered her voice. "Baby, is that Richard's baby you're carrying?"

"No ma'am. It's not. He never went that far." I said removing the world from my mother's shoulders. She lowered her head between her legs and let out a huge gasp. I waited for her to look up. She stood and made her way to me. I had never seen so much pain in my fifteen years of life. She was broken in ways that I never knew a woman could be broken.

"I am so sorry that I wasn't there to protect you. I am so sorry that I didn't make you feel like you could come to me. You must understand that I didn't know. I didn't know." She cried. I said nothing as I looked at my feet. "I've moved back to Sheffield, and I want you and that baby with me."

"Mama, I got a home."

"Your home is with your mother. You're a child, Nette. You're a child. You're my child, and maybe that's where you get this foolishness from, but we gotta do something different. Your body is going to do some things you ain't ready for! You need me. Baby, get your things and come live with me. There is no Richard anymore, and there will never be another Richard." She said strongly. I agreed.

I will not say that my mother was unhappy about the pregnancy, probably disappointed is a better word. I had no doubt that she still loved me and getting Richard out of our lives confirmed such to me. She was right. My body went through things I could have never imagined. She helped educate me. Parts of my body hurt that I did not even know existed. I also went though some emotional changes, as hormones raged in my body. I hated the idea that I could not go out with my friends much anymore, but my mother and grandmother felt as if they were on a time clock to prepare me for motherhood.

While the looks and stares form the students, old friends, and teachers stopped bothering me after a while, it was the look on Antonio's face that troubled me most. In fact, there was no look at all. He would not even look in my direction, and it hurt. It hurt deeply. Trying to focus on the life that was ahead, I continued to go to school and take parenting and nutritional classes. I learned the importance of a proper diet, while getting adequate rest.

"Hey." I said as Antonio pulled a soda from the cooler at the back of the store. Clearly, he didn't hear me. I wondered if I should speak louder or perhaps walk to him. I was embarrassed, but what were the odds that we both would end up at the same neighborhood market at the same time. Perhaps it was fate. Perhaps it was God. What if I never got another chance to see him? I knew that I had to speak to him. So, I took a deep breath, and made my way towards the fountain drinks. "Hey!" I said again. He looked at me for a moment and turned to walk away. While it was clear that he wanted to continue walking, he stopped. "You can't even look at me, can you?", I asked, staring at his backpack. He slowly turned to me. We did not speak. We just looked at one another, until we smiled. I felt relieved.

"Young lady, breathe! You have to breathe" The nurse shouted.

"I am breathing!" I screamed as my body fell apart. She wiped sweat from my face. Almost three hours I sat on a toilet in agonizing pain, before I realized that it was time to go to the hospital. My daughter was ready to introduce herself. "Is my Mama here yet?" I asked looking at the nurses. They ignored me.

"Have you picked out a name yet?" The heavy nurse asked. I leaned my head back on the pillow. I wanted my mother. I needed her. A short while later, I became a mother on September 30th, a date that would hold great significance many times throughout my life.

I had never been so physically and emotionally exhausted. I wanted to hide my fears, but I didn't have a clue what to do. How would I know when my daughter was hungry verses sick? I thought I was ready, but now that she was here so many other fears now plagued my mind, but I held her. When I held her, it felt as if she held me more than I could have ever held her. She held me together, and I knew it. Antonio knew it. He placed the sleeping angel in his mother's arms and then returned to my bedside. He smiled. I loved his smile.

"I cannot believe that you're here. I can't believe she's here." I said.

"You thought she was going to stay in your stomach forever?" He laughed.

"I'm talking about your Mama. She's going to hate me when she finds out that's not your baby."

"She's not like that. My Mama loves me, and she loves whatever I love." He said. That did not make sense to me. "I love you and that baby. I told my Mama the truth." He said. I looked at Mrs. Murphy as she held my daughter. She kissed her, held her, and smiled. She was in love. I looked at Antonio.

"You're gonna be my wife, and I'm going to take care of you both." He said. "We're gonna be a family." How could he love me like that? I was fast, I was damaged, I was insecure, and I didn't have a dime to my name. He wanted me, and for the first time I felt wanted. I hated myself for hurting him. He was beautiful, and his relationship with his mother was a work of art. She adored him. So, I found myself at her home often as Mrs. Murphy helped me care for my daughter. I felt confident as a mother when I was near Antonio's family. They didn't treat me as a child as my own family did. Time was nearing for me to return to school, as I had promised my mother and grandmother. However, I refused to go back to school the way I left.

I did not return to my high school. Instead I enrolled at Antonio's high school as a married woman.

"This don't make no sense!" Grandma said pacing back and forth from the stove to the sink. "Now, having a child is one thing, but she don't know the first thing about being nobody's wife. She ain't figured out how to be a Mama yet." She shouted to Mama. I held my daughter as I began to wonder if Mama and Grandma forgot I was in the room. Typically, by this time they would have sent me out of the room so they could go back and forth, but now I was a mother just like them and I wanted to do what was best for my child.

"You don't live in the house with Jeannette every day. I do. She's not the same little girl you used to think was so innocent and easy going. She's stubborn, and she is going to do what she wants no matter what you or I tell her! I'm not gonna fight with her." Mama retaliated.

"She ain't old enough to sign a marriage license! She's barely old enough to drive, and you bout to turn her over to them folks!"

"I ain't turning her over to nobody! She has this child already, and if she has a man who loves her and wants to take care of her, then she deserves that! That's more than any of us had!"

"That boy ain't a man! He ain't no more of a man than she is a grown woman. They're both kids! I don't understand how you or his Mama can approve of this!" Grandma was devastated. I might argue with Mama, but I could never bring myself to argue with Grandma, so I carried the baby outside onto the porch. I reminisced over just a couple years before pleading to be allowed to ride my bicycle from the porch to Mary's house down the street. There I stood, now informing my family that I would have my own husband, family, and my own porch. Antonio had found an adorable house, that we each thought was perfect. If we didn't want to lose the security deposit, then we had to move fast. I don't know if it was guilt over Richard, frustration with me, or belief that I could actually be a respectable mother and wife, but Mama agreed.

I got married and I left my mother's house when I was 16 years old. I was now a mother myself, and I felt marriage was the next step. At that time, my beautiful daughter was about 5 months old. We decided to get married on Valentine's Day. I was undeniably excited. My mother and father were there to witness my union to Antonio. They both had to be present to sign approval due to my age.

Although it was just a mere courthouse wedding, I stood there as a beautiful princess glowing, and grateful. I still remember some of the stares from the courthouse employees as they watched. Antonio stood next to me, as handsome as ever. He pulled the rings from his pockets, and our union became official. In my eyes, our union validated our love, and our family bond.

How could life be so sweet. I was so excited to decorate a home, my home. It was a small two-bedroom home, but it was perfect. The red brick home sat on a hill, and it was my palace. I couldn't cook much other than spaghetti, but he never complained. We would drop off the baby with family as we both headed to school. We even had classes together. The high school faculty hated what we represented, but we were family. We both worked and contributed to the bills. We made love often, and I adored him. His mother absolutely worshipped the baby, and I couldn't help but smile when she held my daughter. I envied the relationship between Antonio and his mother.

"I can't breathe." I struggled to speak. I looked up from the wooden floor as my daughter's tiny feet moved back and forth in the swing. She screamed to no avail. I prayed her screams would alert the neighbors, because I could not scream as Antonio's hand clutched my throat. I prayed that I would not pass out again.

I had to do something. God help me! I knew that this time he would kill me. He knew that he could kill me. I could not allow her to witness her mother's murder. She would be forever scared.

"I'm sick of you!" he screamed. My breath was too short to move. I struggled, and I fought again, but it wasn't enough. The house wasn't enough. The sex wasn't enough. I wasn't enough. Then it happened. The gun fired, and the screaming stopped.

CHAPTER FOUR

Sleeping with Danger

Girls mature faster than boys. This is the age-old story I told myself the morning after the first time Antonio busted my lip. I was sixteen, and we were still practically newlyweds with a new baby. There we sat on the sofa holding Styrofoam paper plates of my attempts at spaghetti, green beans, and garlic toast. While I noticed that something troubled Antonio the moment he entered the house, I figured I wouldn't pressure him. I would just be the good wife, fix his plate, and join him in front of the tv. I would even have passionate and hot sex with him to ease his mind from whatever troubled him. However, somewhere between asking his thoughts on the meal, and informing him of the baby's growth, he punched me in the face sending me to the floor. The hit was so random.

Not to suggest that the attack would have been okay had it not been so random, but had I anticipated it then maybe I could have measured it. Maybe I could have understood or had some sense of a resolution as to what has just occurred. I lost my breath for a few minutes, shocked by what just happened. I rested on the floor until I could pull my thoughts together, the whole time I was crying. My poor heart cracked in half that day. He left for a few hours and then returned with sincere apologies. He told me that he did not know what had come over him. I believed him, so I stayed, loving him no differently. I did not understand why the abuse occurred, or why he acted the way that he did. Maybe it was some type of unexplainable, unimaginable anger that he needed to release. I forgave him that night, but the abuse increased. I was hit, kicked, and choked. I knew that matters were getting worse, not because of the physical abuse, but because I now knew that he was having sex with other women. That told me that the issue was me. He was unhappy with me, and I became afraid. He was stressed over bills, the baby, and our marriage and the only life that gave him peace was not the life in our home. He found security and some sense of a resolution by sleeping around and now selling drugs. Was I ruining his life? There he was just a year ago a normal teenage boy that all the girls wanted, and then he married a girl with a baby that was not even his. Was it my fault? Antonio was becoming a different person right before my eyes, and I did not know what to do. On another occasion, Antonio drove me to one of the darkest roads in the city. The street was pitched black dark, with no lights. He forced me out of the car and made me walk as he knew my fear of the dark. Speeding cars raced around the dark curves with their headlights beaming. I was afraid, trembling, crying, and fearing that the next car that turned the corner would hit me. I continued walking, as I thought of my Grandmother and our walks. I remembered walking to John's Market for a pregnancy test when I lived in Decatur. It never crossed my mind, that I was not afraid of the darkness that night. I had a goal in mind. I needed to learn if I was pregnant, and my goal was more important than my fears. So, I took a deep breath and thought of my daughter who was in the backseat of Antonio's car. I continued walking. A short while later, a car stopped beside me.

"Man, get in the fucking car." I recognized Antonio's voice. I refused to speak, but I returned to the car. I immediately turned to the rear of the car to check on the baby. She smiled at me. I had no control over my ability to avoid smiling when it came to her, so I smiled back. Eventually, we made it home. I carried her from the car, up the steps to the front door, and into the house. I placed her in her crib. The house was silent.

I returned to the living room. Antonio sat on the sofa with the same lost expression draped across his face. I avoided contact.

"You hungry?" I asked. He didn't reply as I continued into the small kitchen. I opened the refrigerator and pulled a ham from inside. I would just make simple ham sandwiches. Perhaps I could just avoid an argument. He made his way into the kitchen and the arguing continued. Antonio's shouting seemed to cause the walls in the house to shake. I tried to ignore him as I continued preparing the food. Within an instant, he pulled the knife from the counter. The kitchen was silent as we made eye contact. I felt my tears building as I knew he was preparing to kill me. I dashed from the kitchen, jumped over the coffee table, and ran from the house. I could feel him nearing me as he held the knife above his head. I cried out for help as I ran through the gravel driveway. I knew that he would and could kill me. He grabbed me, and in that moment slipped on gravel. He fell to the ground as the knife cut my wrist. He looked into my eyes from the ground. Astonished that my lover, my husband, and my best friend had just attempted to kill me; I returned to the house.

I still believed that I needed to be patient with him, so I hid my bruises and covered my scars. Maybe I blamed myself for ruining his life, but I hid my truth from my family and my world. Perhaps it was investable that a day would come in which he would put a gun to my head. I returned from my memories of trauma and looked into Antonio's eyes. They were dark and cold. He hates me. This was my thought as tears raced from my face as Antonio pinned me down. Months of fights, battles, and arguments had climaxed to the moment that he placed his pistol to my head. He moved the weapon and shot into the hardwood floor inches from my face. I screamed.

"Bitch, I will fucking kill you! You don't know who you're fucking with! I told you I ain't messing around!" He raged. I couldn't see straight. "Do you hear me?" He shouted, again returning the gun to my face. I felt the heat from the weapon on my face, and then out of nowhere, he stood and left the house.

Something happened to me at that moment. I felt something in me that I had not felt since I was younger. I felt as if I was losing control of myself. The rest of the night was a blur, but I woke up in the hospital. I was severely dehydrated, exhausted, and struggling with anxiety attacks. I remember most of my hair being out on one side. I was not sure if it was because he pulled it out, or if it was stress related, but I was losing my hair. I rushed to gather my thoughts so that I could present a suitable or fitting story for my family. The children were with my family, and I could not allow anyone to know that I was in the hospital. Antonio made his way to the bed. He sat next to me.

"I don't feel well." I said.

"You think I give a fuck how you feel?" He shouted, grabbing the IV in my arm. I screamed. "I'll snatch this shit right out of your arm." He said. I cried and feared looking at him.

"Why do you hate me so much? What did I do that made you hate me like this?" I cried. He said nothing. He removed his hands from me. Fearing I would call for help, he dashed from the room in an instant.

Antonio always apologized for his poor behavior, and he made me understand that the streets required him to be abusive and hard. If he was going to provide for us and survive the tough streets selling dope, then he could no longer be the soft and weak Antonio that I fell in love with. He explained that he simply struggles to flip off the switch from his street persona to the father and husband I knew him to be when he made it home. I found myself lying to help Antonio hide his devilish deeds. I even hid and got rid of money and drugs during raids by the police. He was my man, and I was going to fight for him. Afterall, I still felt responsible for what his life had become.

For a while, things started to improve. We argued less often, and we almost seemed to have a normal life. My high school teachers seemed to be accustomed to the idea of having married students in their classrooms also. On an afternoon, I made plans to try a new recipe for my family. Antonio and I loaded our beautiful daughter into her car seat and made a run to the local grocery store when we were hit by a careless driver. I panicked, and immediately turned to the backseat to be sure my daughter was safe. She cried and cried. We were rushed to the hospital. I needed Antonio more in that moment than I had ever needed him before. I was afraid. He was afraid. Regardless of what our marriage had become, I needed him, and our child needed him as well. He loved her as his own, and it angered him if anyone behaved or spoke in a way that indicated he was not her biological father. He never left my side. His eyes were weak. It was obvious that he had cried in the hall. He returned and hugged me. He had not hugged me in that way in so long. He lifted the baby into his arms. He kissed her. I felt relieved.

"Well, all seems well. All seems well." The doctor began assuring us before he fully entered the room.

"My baby is okay?" Antonio asked.

"Which one?" The doctor replied. We were confused.

"Huh?", Antonio said.

"Your girlfriend…"

"She's my wife."

"I'm sorry. Your wife is pregnant." The doctor explained before casually walking away. Had I not already been lying down; I would have fainted. I was afraid. I knew that there was no way that I would convince Antonio to leave his street life now with a second child on the way. That meant, his monstrous side was here to stay.

"We're having a baby." He cheered. He smiled. I exhaled.

"What are you worried about? You're married now?" Everyone seemed to say to me. I heard it at school, at home, and even from family. "You're doing it the right way now." I was told. So, eventually I processed that idea and I too believed that I was doing things the all-American way. I was not afraid of childbirth as I had been the first time. I had been through so much in the recent years, that I was just ready to give birth. A few months later, we welcomed a son into our family. He was just as handsome and charming as Antonio. My son was like a miniature angel God had given me. The way that he looked at me made me feel so empowered, special, and healed. From the first moment I saw him I fell in love, and I knew that he would be a great man one day. I knew it. I could feel God's grace when I held him.

The new baby in all his beauty even seemed to ease Antonio's demons in ways that nothing else could, for a while at least. Eventually, Antonio seemingly grew weary of fighting his demons and found it easier to fight me. The abuse resumed.

The abuse rarely occurred when the children were around, and they were young and really did not understand what was going on. I was moving them from place to place or dropping them off with family while I dealt with my mixed-up feelings about Antonio and my future. My family was close by, and they loved seeing the kids. I began spending more time with family and friends to avoid fights with Antonio. At one time I stayed a few nights with a family member. I hated having to rely on others to transport me and the children back and forth wherever we needed to go, but Antonio had taken my car.

Eventually, Antonio agreed that I needed transportation for the children's sake, so he convinced me to come to get the car.

My cousin Zach was several years younger than I was, but I enjoyed him being with me. So, I asked Bruce if he'd take Zach and I to get my car from Antonio. Bruce was a loyal friend and he expressed that he would be happy to help me. We pulled into the driveway.

"What's taking him so long?" Zach asked. I didn't respond. Eventually, Antonio walked from the house to Bruce's car. I refused to step from the car until he showed me the keys. Antonio stood next to Bruce's window. Bruce lowered the window. The next thing I knew, Antonio reached across Bruce into the car and waved a knife at me, reaching for my throat. Zach and I both screamed as blood splattered onto the dashboard. Bruce yelled as he held his arm. I knew that this was the moment that Antonio would kill me. I had to protect Zach. He was all that I could think about in that moment.

As Zach screamed, I opened the car door and pulled him from the back seat. We both raced from the house. We continued running and screaming. A few moments later, Bruce's car arrived next to us.

"Get in!" He said gasping for breath. His arm was split open. I felt as if I would vomit. Blood was everywhere. "I need you to help me get to the hospital."

"Bruce, I'm so sorry. I'm so sorry. I didn't know he was going to do that. I am so sorry."

"STOP IT! I don't need you to apologize for that nigga! Just get in the car. NOW!" Zach looked at me. I will never forget the look in his eyes.

"It's okay. Come on." I assured him that it was safe to get in the car. We escorted Bruce to the hospital where he received 42 stitches and then 42 staples.

I knew at that time that I could no longer hide the abuse from my family. They were astonished about everything that was going on. You must understand that the entire world worshipped and idolized Antonio. So, did I, and I made it easy for them to view him a black prince. You see, I had seen so many men who were horrible in every way that seeing a man who is only horrible in a couple ways confused the hell out of me. Did he love me? Did he hate me? Did he want me? It would have been easier and much clearer had he been a horrible father and a man who I knew did not love me, but this was not the case.

I was growing weary of the beatings, and people were asking questions. I began to leave my house and the kids, and I would seek refuge with family. Antonio was like an Italian mobster, so to take his children from him was crossing a line. There would be retaliation. He would always find me and drag me back home with the children. After a while, it just became easier on the kids for me to just stay. Maybe it was just easier on me.

Just as soon as I decided to stay, the abuse became daily. I was hit, choked, punched, and threatened every day. He promised that he would kill me, and after a while I began to believe him. I began to plan my next escape. I could no longer hide the abuse from the children, and if I ran to my family, he would find me. So, I entered a safe house.

The safe house was developed to keep battered women and children safe. The program came with many rules and restrictions, but

I did not mind. I spent time in class settings with other women who all detailed their own stories and escape from abuse. I was shocked and sickened to think of the evil in men.

It was recommended that women remain in the safe house for about sixty days, but I left after three weeks. I left on my own and returned to the very man I fled. I was addicted to every part of Antonio and I needed him to forgive me for taking his children from him. So, I pled with him to teach me the skills behind selling drugs. I wanted to be his partner in crime in every way. If he could not escape the lifestyle for us, then it made perfect sense for me to join him in the life. For him I would do anything. I would die for him, and he knew it. He was more than my husband. He was my king. He was my god. He also became my father. Antonio taught me how to defend myself against everyone but himself. He taught me the importance of standing up for myself, and he taught me all the things that my father or Richard never told me.

I felt myself changing also, so I understood the emotional disconnect that was needed to live such a life. I did not like the woman I was becoming, but I had to do what I felt I had to do. I prayed to God that I would never get caught, and that my children wouldn't be taken from me. After a while, I just assumed God had me covered. I felt as if I was being flushed down a drain of corruption and I did not know how to stop it. I knew my time was running out. How could I escape this life?

My Grandmother always taught me that no matter how far you stray, or how far you fall- you never stop praying. Well, I did stop praying. But I always felt someone was praying for me.

"I'm praying for you Nettie Pooh", Grandma said. I covered the receiver on the telephone. I did not want her to hear me cry. No one had called me that in years. All I wanted was to feel like Nettie Pooh again. "I'm praying." She said before hanging up the phone. I dried my eyes and began fixing lunch for the children. The phone rang again.

"Grandma, I really need to get lunch ready…"

"You have a collect call from- Antonio" I" I gasped as I looked to the children in their playpen. Do you accept the charges?" The operator's monotone voice questioned.

"No." I said. I hung up the phone. "No".

CHAPTER FIVE

Laughable Love

"How do you feel?" Kiesha asked, entering the kitchen as I washed dishes. I did not reply. From the soapy water, I lifted the knife that was once used by my husband to cut me. Instead of rinsing the knife, I tossed it in the trash can. "Are you okay?" Kiesha stated. I looked at her. Kiesha was a new friend. She was about my age and she also had a child. She did not understand my life to the degree that I felt we had much in common, but I did feel a bit more normal when she was around.

"I don't know how to feel. I don't know how I should feel."

"You should feel relieved. You should feel safe. It's been months!"

"I know that, and maybe a part of me does feel a bit safer, but I.."

"You what? You love him?" She asked folding her arms across her chest and leaning against the refrigerator. I removed the stopper from the sink and let the water drain. "Look. You got those kids in there to think about. How can you still love him after all he put you through?"

"Love doesn't just go away like that. Yes, he did some fucked up things, but I still love him. I feel safer that he's gone, but I still love him. I am angry, but I still love him. He is their father!" I said drying my hands on a towel. I looked into the living room at the children. I felt too ashamed to tell Kiesha that I had been corresponding with Antonio through letters and phone calls. I still told him that I loved him. He assured me of the same. However, with every letter I read and every letter I sent I still felt as if I sent a piece of my self-respect along with the letter.

I was not happy that Antonio had gone to prison, but I could not deny that I felt this was God's way of giving me an escape from the prison I was in. This was a way to clear my mind, and finally take a moment to figure out who I was beyond my mistakes. What did I want in life? Who could I be? While I missed Antonio, I felt as if this was a second chance, and I did not want to squander it away.

My children were young, and they deeply struggled with the void left in their lives by Antonio's absence. When I realized such, I permitted Mrs. Murphy to take the children for visits with him. At first, I was highly skeptical of allowing my children to go to a prison, but I did not want to deprive them of communication with Antonio. While he was a poor husband, I knew that he adored the children. That I could never take away from him. A few months later, I asked Kiesha if she would baby-sit for me.

"I can't tell you how much I appreciate this." I said preparing a couple bottles of milk.

"Girl, no problem. I got you!" She said smiling at the kids. "They got you working evenings now?" She asked.

"No." I said, and I extended the papers to her.

"What's this?" She asked. I said nothing. I gave her a moment to read. She did not read long, before she looked up at me. She smiled and embraced me. I restrained my tears until I saw her tears.

"He should get his papers any day now." I explained.

"You're divorcing Antonio. Wow. That is so good." She exhaled.

"I think I've known for a while that this was coming, but it just took a while for me to get to this point. You know?"

"Yea. I get it. You're young and you have your whole life ahead of you." She assured me. I loved her.

"Thanks for always being so good to me. Now, how do I look?" I asked her as I posed as if I were on the end of a New York fashion runway.

"You have a date already?" She cheered.

"Well, actually we've been seeing each other for a few months. I just didn't say anything because I was so confused about my feelings for Antonio and our marriage. But, I'm at a different place now." I said feeling the world lift from my shoulders.

"You don't have to explain to me." Kiesha said. "Tell me something about him."

"He's a good man. He's nice and very supportive. It just feels good to have a man look at me that way." I said.

"You look amazing." Kiesha stated. I walked away feeling so amazing about myself. My spirit and heart felt great, but my body ached, and the pain was increasing by the moment. The pain in my abdomen first appeared the moment I woke up that morning, but I assured myself that it was nothing. I was too busy to focus on the pain. I was now accustomed to pushing myself through pain. I stepped from the porch in the front yard. Within a matter of moments, everything became dark, and I fell to my knees in crippling pain. Certain I was dying; I began crying and screaming for help. My voice faded over the traffic. The pain increased as the sun shined upon my face. Eventually, I made it to the hospital.

The emergency room doctor informed me that I was experiencing an ectopic pregnancy. I was stunned and frightened, but I pleaded with the doctors to save my baby. I quickly reached for the phone. Swearing Kiesha to secrecy, I called my boyfriend. I needed his support, and he needed to know what was occurring. He never answered my calls. Instead, I learned of my baby's death alone. I did not want my family to know what had occurred. I did not want to hear or experience judgement or ridicule. I just wanted to get home. I was angry that Chad abandoned me at such a time. I thought he cared for me. I made it home from the hospital just in time to accept the final divorce decree in the mail. Chad showed up three days later. His sister had informed him of the baby's death. I did not focus on him. Instead, I read the papers and limped to the bed. I was grateful to have a babysitter that night because I needed a drink more than I needed air to breathe.

That night I began a love affair with alcohol. I found myself sinking further and further into a dark and miserable depression. Chad ignored me and was already in another relationship. While I did not consider my excessive drinking to be a problem, I decided that I needed to pull myself together enough to enroll back into Sheffield High School for my senior year. The pursuit of education always balanced and stabilized me. I was proud of my decision. I stopped drinking as much, and I focused on building a life with the kids. They needed me as their long for Antonio was increasing with every passing day. I believed that they needed a positive male role model. Enter David.

I had not found myself drawn to an older man since Quincy and look how that turned out. So, originally, I was reluctant to give my body and heart to the older David. However, I was insanely lonely, and I did not want to be alone. I was alone in a world I did not understand so I fell for David and forced myself to forget about all the other men of my past. David was seductive, and he seduced the hell out of me. He did not just seduce my body; he seduced my heart and soul as well. The sex was phenomenal. I found myself drawn to the way that he held me following sex more than the sex itself. Although I did not know he had a family when our romance began, I soon learned of such after I fell for him. I knew that he loved his family, but I also knew that David loved me.

Granted, it was given that I could not reveal David to be the father of my child just yet. We had to figure out a plan, and we had to figure out a plan fast. I did not want to cause a war with his other family. We began to make our plans for a future, but the plans did not involve David leaving his family. I did not need that, so I did not request it. I felt ready. Oh, I found myself marveling in the idea of another chance at love. David made me feel protected and safe in a way that no man had done before. We enjoyed one another's company. Although I was still in high school, working two jobs, and raising two children, David and I found our quality time together. We would take long drives and even visit a few clubs together. He was more than my lover. He had become my best friend, and it felt amazing. He only shared our romance with two of the closest people to him, and I did the same. I was thrilled to be able to tell someone about this mighty man of mine.

"You're sprung." Kiesha laughed from the sofa. She drank a beer from a plastic cup.

"Girl, I am not sprung." I lied, then I laughed. "You sure this is how it's supposed to look?" I asked looking into a mirror as I tried on a few maternity outfits Kiesha had gifted to me.

"It's maternity clothes. It ain't that hoochie shit you used to wearing. It's supposed to be loose." She said. We both laughed endlessly.

"Just as long as I can still get my groove on, because you know I can dance." I had to prove my point. It felt so great to laugh. I had stopped laughing for such a long time. David made me laugh again. He gave me reasons to laugh. A few weeks later, at five months pregnant, I graduated high school. Maybe I didn't walk across the stage. I think God carried me across the stage. I cannot explain how proud of myself that I was at that moment. To be honest, I think that was one of the only moments of my life that I honored and saluted myself. This was my victory, and it felt amazing. Everyone counted Nettie Pooh out. They all said that I could never and would never finish high school. That day was like magic to me. I felt like celebrating, and that is what I did. I celebrated ongoingly for weeks. I celebrated with David, I celebrated with Kiesha, and I celebrated with my children. I wanted to be a mother they could be proud of.

"I'm proud of you babe." David said softly. I held the phone to my ear. I knew that when his voice was low, that Cassie was near.

"Thank you." I said as I paced around my living room. I held my womb.

"I'm serious. I want you to know that I'm really proud of you. I'm not just saying that. I'm proud of you and I love you. You know that, right?" He asked me. I had never experienced so many blissful and joyful emotions at once, so I struggled to even know how to process happiness.

"I know. I love you too. Your daughter loves you too." I said.

"Daughter? It's a girl?" He asked anxiously. The doorbell rang.

"It's a girl." I smiled. I knew that he was smiling as well. I walked to the door. "Kiesha is here. After she gets settled in, I'll head to meet you."

"Tell her I said what's up." David said. Damn, this feels good. I thought. I exhaled and opened the door.

"Kiesha, David…." I froze. The phone dropped from my hands, and my life flashed before my eyes. How could this be happening? I had to be dreaming. This could not be my reality.

"Ain't you gonna invite me in?"

"Hello? Hello??" I heard David's voice repeat from the phone near my feet.

Antonio slowly knelt and picked up the phone. I held my womb closer as he stared at my abdomen. He stood and extended the phone to me. "It's for you."

CHAPTER SIX

The New Norm

"God knows I've missed them." Antonio said looking at the sleeping children. I kept the telephone in my hand so that I could be prepared to call the cops at any moment should he attack me. My heart raced so fast. I was certain this was not good for my pregnancy. I stood in the doorway as he stood over the children. I heard him sniff, and I knew that he was crying. How could he be out of prison? Here I was finally establishing a new life, and my worst nightmare had returned. "Can I come back tomorrow when they're awake?" He asked without looking at me. He knew that I would never keep him from the children.

"Call first." I said coldly. He turned and walked from the darkness of the bedroom to me. The light from the hallways shown upon his face. His face was indeed wet with tears. He took another step further and I jumped.

"I just wanted to hug you. I'm sorry." He said.

"What the fuck are you doing here?" I said trying to avoid screaming.

"What? Did you think I got a life sentence? I don't deserve a second chance?"

"Maybe you deserve a second chance from jail but not from me." I explained.

"I get it. I get it. I'm sorry. You're doing your own thing now." He said looking down to my abdomen. "Does he love you?"

"That's none of your business."

"Does he love my kids? That is my business." He looked like a child.

"Antonio, we're divorced."

"I know. I know. I just want to be friends. That's it. I won't interfere with your new life." He said. Just like that, Antonio was back. I agreed to a platonic friendship. We were able to communicate on a much higher level than ever before. There was no more abuse, and we truly became friends again. We began spending time together with the children as decent human beings. I found myself wanting to be in his presence, missing him. I felt as if I was regaining a friendship with the man I knew in the beginning. The children were thrilled to have their father back, as was I for them.

David seemed bothered by my friendship with Antonio, but he never voiced his concerns. We just continued making our plans for our future and our family.

"Nette, I'm going to pick up the kids and take them to dinner Thursday night." Antonio said, dropping off the children.

"Oh okay. We're going to the same pizza place as we all did last week?" I laughed. He didn't respond. I looked at him. "What?"

"I'm taking them to dinner at my girlfriend's house." He said softly. It was obvious that he did not want to hurt me. I felt my heart break.

"That's fine. I don't have a problem with that. I'm glad you have someone. My man and I have to look for baby items next week anyways. You know I'm getting close to the delivery date." I said trying to make myself busy folding the laundry spread across the sofa.

"Nette, you okay?"

"Boy, please. Yes. I am fine." He nodded and closed the door behind him as he left. I found myself crying as I sat on the arm of the sofa. I looked around the quiet house. I took a deep breath.

Everyone around me became increasingly concerned over my levels of stress. David was deeply worried. He constantly reminded me that I needed to try and calm myself from all the stress happening around me. He was right. He was more than right. David had become a lifeline that I depended on more than I even realized. I needed him.

David died a few days later. With less than a month from my delivery date, David lost his life. He was killed in a horrible car accident, and once again my life was completely dismantled by trauma and tragedy. I was crushed beyond words, and my pain ran deep. I felt as if I was losing myself. Did I need alcohol? Did I need my Mama, Grandma, or Antonio? I didn't know what I needed. I just knew that I did not have what I needed to cope with such a loss. My soul broke, and the man I loved was dead and I could not publicly mourn him because of his family. Kiesha warned and advised me to manage my grief, but it was impossible. I felt as if I was trying to swim the Atlantic. The pain was too much, and three days following David's death, I gave birth to his daughter on September 30th, 1994. I was now the mother of three young children, and I was still a teen.

I did not receive many visitors during this hospital stay. I did not want any visitors, but when my Aunt Tasha came to visit it was exactly what I needed. This was a very private moment, and I did not know how to have this moment without David. I cried endlessly from the moment I gave birth. I did not want to send my daughter to the nursery. I wanted to keep her close to me and tell her of her father.

"Your father isn't here, and I am so sorry that you never got the chance to meet him. He loved you, and I'm going to always make sure you know that." The door opened as a strange woman glanced into the room and looked around. She then left the room. I overlooked the strange moment and looked at my daughter. "You have a big sister and a brother who are always going to look out for you also." I kissed her head, and I swear that she smiled. The strange woman returned and held the door open. "Can I help you?" I asked as she held the door open for another woman to enter. While I had never seen her before, the moment her face appeared in the light; I knew who she was. The expression on her face was clear. Her eyes were dark. She had an angered look on her face. My heart skipped. It was Cassie. She spoke.

"Why are you doing this?"

"Look. I don't know what you..."

"Why are you lying about this fucking child?" She shouted. I held my daughter closer. I looked around for a button to call for help.

"I don't want to cause any problems." I began to cry.

"You have already caused problems! You are tarnishing David's reputation with lies that he is her father! Stop what you are doing! We are a family! We were a family, and you should have respect for me during this time."

"You should have respect for me! This is his child. I didn't tell anyone because I didn't want to hurt anyone."

"Stop lying to me!" She screamed as she rose her hand above her head. I feared she would attack us. "That is not his baby. Keep his name out of your mouth, and if you even think of showing up at his funeral with that baby, then…." She looked into my eyes. She raged as we both wept. She walked away. The door closed behind her as I heard her sobs echoing throughout the halls.

I refused to allow my daughter to go to the nursery that night as I learned Cassie was a nurse at the hospital. Instead, I immediately hatched a plan to prove the paternity of my child. As soon as I took the baby home, I began the pursuit of proving David was the father of my baby. The state kept record of David's blood from the car wreck, which was used to establish paternity. I was aware that Cassie would receive the decree of paternity, but I had no idea that it would happen on the day of the funeral. I felt horrible for Cassie and her child. I felt as if the entire world hated me, and in that moment, I began to hate myself.

I was summoned to court where I had to testify and give personal accounts of my relationship with David. I felt humiliated. David's family did not appear for court, but my mother sat in the courtroom as I spoke. I would not allow his family to make me hide the truth. I did not have much to give my children, but the truth was free. They would always have my truth. Eventually, a few of his family members finally accepted her as their blood, while many others refused.

I struggled to love myself following what I believed to be such great wrong. My daughter wasn't wrong, but my disregard for someone else's love kept me up at night. To silence the pain, I returned to drinking heavily. I began to wonder if Antonio would give me another chance. I was a single mother of three children, and I needed help in every way possible. I knew that I was toxic. I was toxic towards everyone, including myself. I was spiraling out of control, with no ability to control, understand, or master my own demons. I knew nothing of coping skills and the ability to manage my emotions in a healthy way. I didn't even know what healthy looked like. You see, I grew up seeing so many strong people, but they were not healed people. I made the mistake of thinking that the ability to keep going meant that I was fine. In reality, I was not fine. My soul was aching and the only way I knew to feed my soul was by feeding my body. I fed my body men. The grief of David's death consumed me. My life was becoming a revolving door of men, and I was sinking. In the midst of so much agony, it seemed like almost overnight I found myself on the delivery table again. I gave birth again to another son from just another relationship. It was not at all my intention to bear a child from this relationship, but it did happen.

I didn't have time to focus on my newest child's father, because when my water broke weeks before my due date, I did not know what to expect. After hours of labor and delivery I had the motherly pleasure of bringing another son into the world. Usually when a mother delivers a child, she gets to hold him, kiss him, and feel the excitement of her child being in the world. However, during this delivery, something was different. My son was not moving, he was not crying, I was not able to see him or hold him. I was scared stiff.

Without hesitation my son was placed into an incubator and taken away from my presence. Being confused, upset, and overwhelmed, I cried out about what was happening. He was transported to a hospital in a different city to receive special care. After a couple of days, I was able to go to the hospital and visit my son. When I finally saw him, I felt complete. He brought a special kind of peace to my life and a special smile to my face. He remained in the hospital. I never missed a visit, and I always continued to show him love. After a couple of weeks of him being on a respirator, I brought him home to join his other three siblings. The other children adored him as did I. I was happy that my son was home and well. For the next few months, he seemed to be making progress. Soon after, I noticed a delay in his crawling. When he would crawl, but he would drag one side of his body behind him. He appeared to be in pain. I also noticed a delay in his speech, with continuous drooling. He also had a problem holding his head steady. I immediately addressed these issues to the doctors.

There were so many sleepless nights when my son would cry in pain, and I did not know where the pain was coming from. I spent nights holding him, rocking him, and kissing him just to bring him some type of comfort. We traveled to many doctors, getting one opinion after another. We spent numerous days and nights in hospitals in different cities. After several months, I finally got the information that I longed for. I was informed that sometime during my pregnancy, or during delivery, my son had a stroke. This information gave the doctors a course of direction and treatment needed so that my son could begin to progress. I took him home. My peace was robbed. I feared losing one of my children. I needed someone near to me, and whenever I felt lonely, I knew what I longed for; but I did not have it. I was alone.

When Antonio pulled away and stayed away for months at a time, I knew that I was alone. He had returned to a life of crime, and he avoided us to avoid bringing the dangers of his life back into our lives. I respected that, but I missed him. I think I still wanted him. I sank further into a depression when Mrs. Murphy died. She was a lovely woman who held such a dear place in my heart and the hearts of my children. I hated that I could not grieve with Antonio. Everyone watched helplessly as Antonio spiraled out of control. The loss of his mother consumed him in every way that a man could be consumed. His hope was gone.

As I struggled to put the pieces of my life together, tragedy struck again. I will never forget the morning when my dear friend Ashley arrived at my home informing me that Antonio had been murdered. Only four months following the death of his mother, Antonio had been shot multiple times, and he left us. I screamed uncontrollably. I informed my children that Antonio was dead, and they were equally devastated. My heart was broken. Every time in my life that I believed that my heart could not suffer greater heartache, life proved me wrong. I got in my car and drove to the house where he had died. Bullet holes and blood spread throughout the home. Photos of my children were gone. Antonio's death was horrible in every way. He had spiraled down such a path of crime and corruption that his final breath was taken in a shootout with police.

While already being accused of many crimes and possibly murder, Antonio had begun abusing other women. I was told that the mother of Antonio's most recent girlfriend had called the police to report that he had beaten her daughter. Antonio had long expressed that he would always go down in a blaze of glory before he would return to prison. So, when the police arrived, he hid himself in the attic of his home. Fighting the fumes of tear gas, he refused to give in. The moment the authorities entered the attic the shootout began, and Antonio was killed.

I had no ability to manage my grief, and I found myself in the comfort of Omar. He adored me, and I needed that. I allowed Omar to spoil me for many months because I had never been spoiled before. But when I learned that I was pregnant again I knew what had to be done.

"Thanks for meeting me." I said leaning against my car. He sat on the hood of his car as he smiled. He was so wholesome and charming. Omar did not drink much at all, he didn't smoke, or even curse. He adored me, but I knew that I would never and could never do right by him.

"We breaking up?" He asked suddenly.

"What? What makes you think that?"

"I don't know. Don't tell me that you're tripping again?" He said exhaling.

"I'm not tripping about anything. What does that supposed to mean?"

"I don't know. You're the one who asked to meet in this empty parking lot in the middle of the day to talk. What's so important that we couldn't talk over the phone?" He asked, raising one eyebrow higher than the other.

"My kids are home. I didn't want them to hear me on the phone."

"They're always home when we're on the phone. What's the big deal with that now?"

"Omar, I'm pregnant." I said as he started getting on my nerves. He tilted his head and he looked at me.

"For real?"

"I have kids. I think I know when I'm pregnant." I said folding my arms. He stood from the hood of his car. He exhaled again and looked at me. He was so naive to the world that I lived in.

"Cool. You think it's gonna be a boy or girl?" He asked.

"What? Nigga, I don't know. What type of question is that?"

"It's a commonsense question. You're pregnant. Ain't that the first thing people wonder when they get pregnant?"

"They wonder that when they want to know. I don't want to know because I'm not going to be pregnant long enough to find out." I explained. There was a silence.

"You want to have an abortion? What if I don't want you to have an abortion?"

"Are you gonna carry the baby? No! It's not your decision." I snapped.

"Then why did you call me? Why am I here if you have already made your mind up?" He said angrily.

"I can't do this again, Omar! I can't have another child. I'm tired. Please." I said as my voice faded. "Now, I could have kept this from you."

"Don't act like you're doing me a favor! I get it. You want me to pay for the abortion even though I may want the child."

"Do you want the child, Omar?"

"Nette! I don't know! You just sprung this on me thirty seconds ago. Can I think for a minute?"

"There ain't no reason to think. I'm sorry. I'm doing this, and I have two jobs. I can pay for it myself." I said looking at the car seats in my car.

"Then why are you telling me any of this? What do you want from me?" He shouted.

"I'm scared!!! I don't want to do this alone." I raged, as I cried. We were silent. He looked at me. "I don't have anyone else, Omar."

"Okay. Okay." He said, and he hugged me.

Omar was more of a boyfriend than some of my husbands had been husbands to me. Whatever he was, I was not ready for him to be another man to whom I shared a child. Granted he was caring, and charming, but I had made a promise to myself. I was already the mother to four children. We drove to the women's clinic.

I left my car and rode with Omar. I did not want anyone in town to recognize my car in the parking lot of the women's clinic. The moment we arrived it all began. There were protestors ranting and shouting at me. They scolded me with scriptures and threats of my soul burning in hell. I walked quickly with my head down low. By the time I entered the lobby, I exhaled. The lobby was small, and there were a few women there waiting. Omar stood next to me as I waited at the sign in the window. The two women who waited gave me different looks. While one woman looked at me with admiration for having a man accompany me to the clinic, the other woman seemed to be angered that Omar was with me. The lady told me the price and I turned to Omar. He looked into my eyes, but eventually placed the money onto the countertop. I suggested he take a seat while I speak to the lady at the front desk. Omar sat nervously. I was given a clip board with forms, and I sat next to Omar as I completed the forms. I then returned the forms to the woman at the window. The waiting seemed to go on forever. Omar and I did not speak to one another as we waited, but the moment they came for me he jumped to his feet. I left him in the lobby as I made my way into the procedure room. As I anticipated, the room was sterile and cold.

I was instructed to remove my clothes and to put on a paper gown. I did as instructed, and within a few moments I was on the table staring at the head of the doctor and nurse. The doctor and nurse informed me that I would feel a strong suction and it would all be over.

They continued talking and laughing on other matters unrelated to me or the disaster occurring before them. I felt embarrassed. They made the entire procedure feel so casual. Just as they explained, there was a loud vacuum noise, a pain, and I was pregnant no more. I dressed, and slowly walked to the lobby. Omar ran to me. He hugged me. He kissed me on my forehead, and we walked from the building. The protestors were gone to my relief. I could not have faced them again.

Following the abortion, guilt now joined my daily struggles with grief, and self-hate. I wrestled with nightmares of the abortion. When drunk, I would hallucinate of seeing the baby. I wondered who the child might have grown up to be. Sadly, within a matter of months Omar and I found ourselves at the women's clinic again. I was ashamed. I was humiliated. I could no longer look Omar in the face, so I ended the relationship. It had to be done. I knew that I could not give him what he truly wanted and needed from me.

Almost a year following Antonio's death, I still grieved horribly, and nothing filled the void. I needed something different this time. I did not need another baby daddy, I needed more. I needed and craved love. So, I found and married husband number two almost a year following Antonio's death. Enter Juan.

Juan was a good and honest man and I was determined that I would make it work with him. However, he saw me as troubled, and I saw myself as perfectly fine. I was a mother of four children, and I had just entered the first year of my second marriage, so I felt as if I was making significant progress. So, what if I was drinking more, partying more, and out of my fucking mind most of the time. I came home at night. I cooked dinner. I bathed, cleaned, and fed my children and I had sex with my husband as I believed I was supposed to do.

Over the recent weeks, I had called Quincy's mother. Antonio was dead and I began to feel as if I should allow my oldest daughter to meet her paternal family and her father. She was seven or eight years old at the time, and I refused to lie to her. While Antonio loved her as his own child while he was living, she was not his daughter. Her father was the man who took my virginity. I had thought of contacting Quincy several times during Antonio's incarceration, but now the time was presenting itself.

So, I explained to my beautiful daughter about her father. I packed her clothes, and we made the drive to her paternal grandmother's home. I felt a bit awkward being in the presence of Quincy's family after so many years, but I could tolerate it for my daughter. I knelt to my daughter and kissed her on her forehead as I said goodbye. She would spend an entire week with Quincy's family. I said a prayer and drove away. That seemed to be the longest week of my life, but eventually I picked her up and we went home. My precious angel wasted little time informing me that her father had touched her private parts. I was stunned. I was outraged. Quincy molested my baby; his mother knew of it and I wanted to kill him. I tried to gather myself. I never wanted her to feel as I felt when Richard sexually assaulted me. I assured her that she would never see her paternity family again.

Juan had big goals and dreams for our family, but by this time my dreams were dead. I just needed relief and peace. Juan was an angel, and sadly enough I did not know how to love a healed and whole man. He grilled me over partying and the excessive drinking. Time and time again he poured all his love and efforts into our marriage and caring for me and my children. However, I could never get myself to love him as deeply as I loved Antonio. I think that he knew my heart rested with another man. Juan worked to teach me matters of business, finances, and growth. I had no interest. I found myself entertaining other men, and I knew that Juan could never forgive me. I knew that he could never trust me again. He was unhappy, and that could not be denied.

Due to my foolish and unsettling behaviors, Juan and I soon divorced. I missed Antonio, and perhaps I missed him so much that I made the incredibly foolish decision to marry an all new version of the worse parts of Antonio, named Andre. So, six months following my divorce from him, I married my third husband. Enter Andre.

Back then I did not understand that while I mastered changing all the external components of my life, everything internal remained damaged. So, it was only fitting that I would marry another version of Antonio.

Like many others, I genuinely thought I loved Andre. I did love him as much as a traumatized woman with my baggage could have loved a man at that point in her life. No man had hit me since Antonio, but there I was again the victim of my husband's physical and emotional abuse. However, Andre went to prison six months following our wedding for a crime he committed before we were married. He stayed in jail for about twelve months while I took care of the kids. I was miserable and again, alone. We communicated through letters, but I longed for more. I longed for Andre and his embrace.

Eventually, Andre was transferred to the local work release where he was still in custody but received many weekend or evening passes in which he came home to me and the children. I enjoyed our reunion for a while, until the abuse started again. I felt as if I failed myself waiting for Andre's weekend passes to be released from the work release just to come home and kick my ass. He was bitter towards me and I knew it.

The older children began seeing the violence and I knew that I had come too far from nights like this with my first husband to tolerate this again. I refused to repeat such a lesson again as if I had not already learned how this would play out. I knew that I had to get away. A holiday was nearing, and I knew that Andre would not be home for several days. I could not suffer at his hand any longer. It was time for me to flee Sheffield, and that is what I did. I loaded the children up and we escaped to Oklahoma.

I immediately felt peace my first night in Oklahoma. My heart was not racing, and even the children seemed at peace. I exhaled in a way that I had not done in so long.

"Thank you for taking us in. I can't tell you how much this means." I said pulling the blankets across my children. I sat on the edge of the bed and looked at them all. When did I birth four children? It seemed as if it was just yesterday that I was begging Grandma to let me ride bikes with Mary. I thought to myself.

"I'm just happy to help. They deserve better than that." He said. I looked at him. He continued. "Nette, you deserve better than that."

"Thank you, Juan. Thank you." Re-enter husband number two.

CHAPTER SEVEN

The Suffrage

We remained and recuperated in Oklahoma for several months. Eventually the phone rang.

"How do you like Oklahoma?" Andre said coldly. My legs weakened. He found me. "You know you can't run from me, right? Bring your ass home, before I come out there and get you. Trust me. If I have to come all the way to Oklahoma it's gonna be worse. Get the fuck home now!" He threatened.

I felt helpless. Although he was hundreds of miles away, I felt as if he was standing before me. I refused to follow his instructions. But after he changed his approach, I compromised and made plans to return home. I moved in with my cousin while I searched for a home. I refused to keep running. Andre was still in work release, but he promised to do better. I believed him, or maybe I just believed what I felt I needed to believe. I was tired of being alone. Afterall, he was my husband. My optimism was indeed short lived. Needing to feel validated myself, I brought TJ into my bed. I wasted no time having sex with TJ.

While I had always been attracted to older men, TJ was younger, and he blew my mind. In walked this fine, sexy, suave, and confident young man and he blew my mind and my body. Now, I wasn't old myself, but I felt old. I had been through a lifetime of drama that women in their nineties hadn't experienced. I had so much responsibility, that TJ reminded me what it felt like to be young, wild, and free. So, I freely gave myself to him. By this time Grandma began. dealing with health issues, so I would regularly check in on her when I was not swamped with the kids. When I realized how much she needed me, I began trying to make time in my schedule to assist her without neglecting my children. However, before I could begin my efforts to help Grandma, I learned that once again, I was pregnant. Andre was still in work release, but I knew that TJ was the father. I felt silly and irresponsible to have to tell him that he would be a father. There I was married, but pregnant by another man other than my husband. He was so young. He accepted the news of an expected daughter and became excited about the idea. By this time, I had already had four other children, lost a child, and had abortions, so pregnancy was no big deal to me.

    I informed my children that I was pregnant and that I needed their help around the house. They seemed shocked about another addition. Truth be told, everyone seemed shocked. Even Andre seemed shocked and excited in his own way, or at least interested in claiming the child as his own.

    "How in the hell do you keep getting these men to be okay with you being pregnant by someone else?" I kept hearing this question. It was not flattering. It made me feel small and insecure. I felt that at any minute Andre would open his eyes and leave me. I would only see Andre on weekends when he would get a pass to leave the work release. Andre begged me to forbid TJ from claiming paternity so that we could raise the child ourselves. The pregnancy was difficult because I contracted gonorrhea from TJ which led to regular hospital stays while I fought to keep the child. Andre urged me to cut TJ out of the picture. Even though I knew TJ now had a new girlfriend, I refused to meet Andre's demands. I did not agree with such, so when I went into labor, Andre and TJ both angrily paced the floors of the hospital waiting to see my new baby girl. As if I was not wrestling with enough emotions, I learned that Juan had remarried. Juan married Kiesha and I was beyond furious. I had never felt such betrayal. I was angry and I wanted to show my anger, but I put my focus on my children and the most important issue at hand.

Several people began questioning the paternity of my youngest child. Did I conceive her during a weekend pass with Andre, or was TJ truly her father? I agreed to do a paternity test, and TJ was confirmed to be her father. Andre and I soon divorced. While we did not divorce because of the paternity revelation, we could not remain married. I could not continue the abuse. Andre pleaded with me to allow him to serve as her father, but I refused. I often feared that I robbed her of Andre's love even though he was not her father. Alright. There I stood in my truth. I had three marriages down the drain, and five children. David and Antonio were both dead, and Quincy was a child molester. Considering the fact that Quincy was an adult and I was a child when our relationship began, perhaps I should have found it to be of no great surprise for him to be such a vile character. However, I did not focus on his behavior as much as I did assuring my daughter that I would never let him hurt her again.

I felt as if I was more of a failure following this divorce than I had ever felt when my other marriages ended. Perhaps at this point in my life, I not only felt as if I failed as a wife, I felt as if I failed my children. I did not know how to handle those emotions. I told myself that I was done with the idea of settling down. I would never again allow a man to make empty promises to me. I promised myself that I would never again put myself in a position to be let down by a man. This time would be about me. I needed to learn how to smile again on my own, and I needed to just enjoy myself. I needed to have fun. I was so damned tired of a million responsibilities.

When I learned that TJ was dead, I felt more of an urge to free myself. He had spent some time in a wheelchair following being shot. His health declined fast, and I had to tell another one of my children that their father was dead. So again, I was thrown into the darkness of grief.

I was tired of all the pressure, even though I adored my children. I was tired and I needed to relax. I can still remember the moment that I managed to flip off my emotions. It was almost as if I flipped a light switch. I knew when it was necessary for me to flip the switch back on, but for the most part, I left my emotions turned off. So, with my emotions off, I was ready to live. I shortened my hair and I shortened my skirts and I became known as the life of every party. It wasn't a party until Nette walked in, and my face was always in the place. I found myself selling my body to men for the cash to take care of my children.

The hot, sexy, and intoxicating night life was now a part of my everyday life. If there was excitement, people, alcohol, and music, I was there. Drinking, dancing, and laughing, I felt as if I was on fire. I was hot! I hung out a lot, mainly at clubs. I would also go to parties, bootleggers, and bars, but no matter where I was, I refused to go home until I felt free. I had my first drink with a group of friends when I was about 17 years old, but now I could drink anyone in the bar under the table. My drinking was relentless, consuming over twenty drinks in single nights, and then driving home to my children. One would think that even after losing two dear friends to driving while under the influence, that such a tragedy would have had an indirect awakening on me, but it did not. I was stronger and more capable than that. I wasn't suicidal, but I was careless with my life.

And at the end of the night or that next morning, I would always be thankful that I made it to my destination safely. I fell in love with Gin, as I began to hide bottles throughout my house, car, and even my purse. I refused to believe that I was an alcoholic. I was a mother, and I still did my job. I functioned fine during the day, but night was my time. As long as I woke up and performed as nothing was wrong, then there was no problem and I did not want to hear anyone's conflicting opinion of my life.

The more fun I had during this time the more I realized that I never had a chance to be young and free. I figured that I could be free during graveyard hours as long as I made it home to my children before morning. Men fawned over me, and it felt awesome rejecting them when I felt like rejecting them. It felt even better accepting them when

I felt like accepting them. I was in control of my life, and I had made a promise to remain in control. I accepted an invitation to attend a party at a bootlegger's house. I needed to unwind, and my girlfriend Stacey was always there to help me do so. She promised me that she would be the designated driver. I got dressed, and we headed out for the night.

"Damn girl. You ain't wasting no time, are you?" A voice said from behind me as I flopped down on a leather recliner. The coolness of the leather felt perfect on my skin. I turned my head to see him. Enter Malcolm.

"You talking to me?" I asked.

"Yes. I told my friends that I'm only talking to beautiful women tonight. Since you're the only one I see, then we have a lot to talk about." Just like that I smiled. He was cute, and I could not remember the last time a man flirted with me. I had sex with men who had never flirted with me. I married men who had never flirted with me, but Malcolm was old school suave. I think that he knew from my first laugh that he had me. I think I knew it as well.

I was immediately attracted to his smile, appearance, and charisma. This man was smooth talking and remarkably interesting. I received a phone call from him the following day and our journey began. We stayed in different cities, but still managed to spend time together. I would drive to see him, or he would drive to see me. I kind of enjoyed having a new man that was not of my regular circle or town. During our conversations and visits, we steered off track somehow. Several months into the relationship we broke up. I wasn't quite sure what went wrong, but I was focused more on taking care of Mama and

Grandma. So, I had no time to put up a fight to save a relationship. My mother had been terribly ill the last few years. I would take her to doctor appointments and to see specialists as often as possible. Her doctors were having a hard time figuring out what was going on with her. She didn't have insurance for quite some time during her sickness. She was finally awarded her disability, but by this time her illness was irreversible. I watched her struggle to take care of herself. Each time I would see her she seemed weaker. I had my hands full, but somehow Malcolm and I still found our way back to each other. Once again, we were driving back and forth to see each other.

By the time, the year 2009 came around, I had relaxed my rule on marriage. So, I married Malcolm as my fourth husband. There we were in one house, together, and over time my children became attached to him. Early on I became aware that he had health problems that would eventually get worse over time. The stress of his health issues brought out parts of Malcolm that troubled me. I knew that he loved me, but verbal and emotional abuse began to creep from the shadows of our love. I became increasingly concerned with his health, and his excessive drinking. Yes. I battled with drinking as well, but never to the point of causing any confrontation that would harm our marriage.

I became pregnant with my sixth child. After child number five, I refused to have any further children. Malcolm changed that. I wanted to give him a child. I wanted to share that bond with him. So, while my older children were practically adults themselves, I was starting again with motherhood. I became excited about the pregnancy.

Mama and Grandma were both in the same nursing home, so I regularly spent time there. I proudly told Mama that I was pregnant.

"Well, Nettie Pooh. I know you'll be fine." She said from her bed. She was weak. I sat next to her. I expected her to say more. "Baby, have you visited with your Grandma?"

"I'm going to go see her next."

"You need to be closer to her, baby. She loves you Nettie Pooh." I nodded.

"Yes ma'am."

"I can see it now. That baby is gonna be a boy. A fat ole' light skinned boy." She laughed and smiled. It felt so good to see her smile.

Malcolm took care of the children as I knew I had to be near my mother. I knew that her time was running out. I camped out at her bedside for weeks, months, and I refused to leave her. It broke my heart to see her in such pain and agony. She moaned often, and it troubled my soul. I was not ready for what I knew was coming. I wondered if God could be answering my prayers. I entered Mama's room as she looked out of the window. She was quiet. I knew that she already knew. She spoke.

"Well, they say my Mama died today." She said without turning her head from the window. I knew that she was crying. I did not know what to say. I did not want to cry, but Grandma was gone. I held my womb. "Well, I guess I won't be long behind her."

"Mama, don't say that." I said rushing to her. I sat on the bed next to her. She eventually looked at me. I had never seen that look on her face. Her heart was broken. Everything that she was to me, Grandma was to her.

"My Mama is gone." She cried. I wrapped my arms around her.

"Mama, I love you. I'm so sorry for being all the wrong things that I have been. I'm so sorry for saying all the wrong things that I have said. I'm so sorry for it all." I wept.

"You don't have to tell me you're sorry. I just want to know you and those babies are gonna be taken care of when I'm gone."

"Yes ma'am."

"Nettie Pooh?"

"Ma'am?"

"Baby, I just need you to do one thing for me."

"Yes?" I asked, holding her hand.

"Don't let me die alone. I don't want to die alone." I pulled her frail body into my arms. I removed her from the nursing facility and had her transported home. Two weeks later I watched as my mother took her final breath.

I felt lost and alone. There were people around me. My children were near me. Malcolm was near me, but I felt alone in a world that was much too big for me. The only two people that I truly knew loved me were gone in a matter of two weeks. I felt like the grief was unbearable, and my pregnancy became increasingly difficult. I felt as if I failed them both. I feared that they both slipped away from me before I became a woman, they would have been proud of. The idea of having to continue life without my mother devastated me.

On September 30th, the joyful date previously known to me as the date I celebrated the births of two of my daughters, I watched my mama take her final breath. It felt as if my entire childhood died with her. I was asleep on the couch next to her bed. I heard what I thought was her trying to talk to me. However, it was her taking her last breaths. I was devastated and my mind and body struggled to handle the loss.

I delivered my son February 7, 2011. The pregnancy was incredibly difficult. My son and I almost died during delivery. He spent 2 weeks in the hospital on a ventilator before being released to go home. Three months later I suffered a long coming mental breakdown. I found myself completely void of the ability to speak. I could speak no words. We were concerned I had suffered a stroke or worse, but doctors insisted my shut down was a mental break.

Before long, I was back home with all my children, but continuing with marriage and the verbal and emotional abuse. Malcolm's health issues, the abuse, along with the drinking, our marriage began to take a turn for the worse.

When my son was about a year old, Malcolm and I separated, and he took the baby with him. Soon after he got his own place for them. However, the baby spent a lot of time with family that would become his godparents. They kept him for extended periods of time. Even with us being separated, we still drove back and forth to see each other. I was faithful in assisting him with his doctor appointments, medications, and hospital stays. I sometimes went days without even leaving his hospital room. I would go to his house and spend days and nights to make sure that he and my son had the things they needed.

During all of this I started a relationship with another man named Roger. I somehow told myself this was okay because me and my husband were separated. I was torn between two men, but I always put my husband and child first. Maybe this is why my husband was so bitter towards me. I feel like I tried everything that I could to make things work. No matter how hard I worked to help take care of him, he continued with the verbal, emotional, and then financial abuse. We argued and said very harsh words to each other. No matter how poorly we spoke to the other, I continued to grocery shop, pick up meds, go to doctor appointments, and even clean Malcolm's vomit, urine, and feces. While there was something so nasty and mean about him, there was also a loving, caring side to him that I genuinely loved. I knew that his inner demons had nothing to do with me, much like my demons had nothing to do with him. However, our demons could not coexist in the same space no matter how much we loved one another.

His kiss and warm touch continued to draw me in each time that we were together. Roger could not change that, so we eventually broke up. I found myself struggling to make ends meet and provide for my children. I knew that I had no one else but myself. Malcolm was not assisting me financially, so I had to take care of everything. Throughout my own personal financial struggles, Malcolm made sure the needs of our son were met. Many people criticized me for allowing my son to live with Malcolm. They felt as if I should have my son with me and my other children. However, I knew that Malcolm was only fighting for his life for his son. I couldn't take that away from him.

As time went on the tension increased with Malcolm's family. Each time that he would fall gravely ill I was around. I was accused of trying to kill him. Per his medical conditions, I knew when something wasn't right with him and I always knew when to take immediate action. I can only assume that he spoke negatively about me to his family that caused them to have these misconceptions about me.

However, my husband just asked me to keep the peace. Oh yes, I humbled myself in more ways than one. A while later, we divorced. We agreed on everything that was listed in the divorce, even down to the soul parental custody of our son. Did I sign over my rights like some people think? Why, hell no. I couldn't take the emotional pain anymore. Shortly following the divorce, Malcolm became gravely ill again. I rushed to his aide, and he welcomed me. After the divorce, his family truly became nasty towards me. They stopped referring to me by my name, and only addressed me as *ex-wife*.

When I visited the hospital, I was not permitted to enter the room to visit by myself. There were a few incidents when the family told the nurse not to let me in at all. Already completely struggling to feed my children, I quit my official final job to provide better care for the man to whom I was no longer married.

Even after the divorce we tried to get back together. I was too emotionally and mentally unstable to deal with his behavior and his family. I feared another breakdown coming on.

The following January, Malcolm died. I got a phone call during the late-night hours as he would call sometimes, so I assumed it was him calling. It was his daughter letting me know that he was in the hospital. I was about fifteen minutes into the drive to the hospital when a cold chill crossed my spine. I knew that Malcolm was dead. I began grieving immediately. I was absolutely devastated. His family told me that I had no right or reason to grieve.

During my grieving process, I would cry uncontrollably sometimes feeling as if I was about to lose my breath. I stared at my phone. Repeatedly, I read Malcolm's last text message to me that read: *I still love you; Wifey.* Once I got to the hospital, my instincts were true. Malcolm was gone. The night of Malcolm's death, I immediately got my son, and brought him home. Our new journey began. We had to learn new things about each other. However, I became depressed and overwhelmed with everything that was going on surrounding my ex-husband's death. I found myself praying on my knees, that God would not allow me to suffer another breakdown. With tears dropping to the floor like great raindrops, I pled for my sanity. I became suicidal and homicidal and was admitted to the psych ward at the hospital. I literally felt like my soul was leaving my body. Lord, how am I going to make it through? I pled.

I wrestled with thoughts that my children would be better off without me. I felt as if I had spent so many years hurting so many people. Amid my agony, I still longed for Malcolm. I needed and wanted to be close to him. I felt as if I was losing the feelings that he once gave me, and I didn't know how to maintain those feelings. Even when I was released from the psychiatric ward, I still felt a yearning in my spirit to connect to Malcolm. Of all the men that occupied time and space in my life, I believed that there was some purpose from God pertaining to my relationship with Malcolm.

I felt a sense of being lost that I had never experienced before. I was tired of so much. I was tired of being tired. For a few days I had a yearning to visit a specific bootlegger's house. While it was not at all abnormal for me to be in such a place, the yearning to be at a specific house was overwhelming me. I could not shake the feeling. I ignored the feeling for some time and told myself that it was just the devil trying to tempt me down further paths of dismay. However, something on the inside of me felt compelled. Eventually, I gave in.

Now I had been to many bars, clubs, and bootleggers throughout my now forty plus years of life, but this time was different. I was not going to find love, sex, men, or even alcohol. I was going to find me. My friend Stacey and I entered, and I felt out of place. That shocked me immediately. I felt more at home in these places than I often felt in my own home. But there we sat. Stacey became concerned with my abnormal behavior. She did not know how to help me, but she offered me a drink. She immediately assured me that I did not have to drink unless I wanted to. Of course, I drank. I appreciated her so much. I began to reminisce of meeting Malcolm in a setting remarkably similar, and I felt warmth. I felt comfort. I felt him.

I closed my eyes to absorb the moment into my soul. I exhaled. My moment was disturbed as a commotion grew across the room and over the music.

"What's going on?" I angrily asked while looking around.

"Beats me." Stacey replied. "Hey, what's all that noise about?" Stacey asked, pulling on the sleeve of a woman who passed us.

"Child, Henry Lee done made it. Them fools act like he's some celebrity or something." She said as she continued towards the back of the room. I looked at the woman as she walked away. She was Mama's age if not older. I felt saddened for her. I did not want to be her age still seeking men, peace, and purpose in such a place.

We looked towards the crowd in the dark corner as the laughing increased. As expected, Henry Lee made his way to our table as soon as he sniffed the new meat in the room. I felt my eyes rolling in my head before he spoke. I lifted my drink to my mouth. I was not in the mood for this.

"What's happening Lil' Mamas?" Henry Lee said standing over my table. We did not speak. In fact, we did not even look up to him. He spoke again, and this time he quickly rendered my attention.

"Girl, it's amazing how much you look like your Mama." I lowered the glass from my face and focused my eyes on him. Stacey looked at me. "You're lil' Nettie Pooh, ain't you?"

"Who the fuck are you?" I asked.

"Nette." Stacey said. She knew how quickly my temper could rise. Henry Lee hesitated.

"Uncle Henry."

"I ain't got no goddamn Uncle Henry so move on."

"I'm Richard's brother. Henry. I ain't seen you since you were a little girl." He explained. I felt as if all the oxygen was sucked from the room. The old man's smile faded as he looked at me.

"Nette, baby what is it?" Stacey asked. I spoke.

"You ain't my Uncle because that mutha fucker ain't my Daddy!" I screamed. The music stopped and the room was silent. Stacey looked around. I found myself standing.

"Well, I know Richard ain't your real Daddy, but you ain't gotta disrespect him. He loved you…"

"Don't you dare finish that sentence. You don't know shit about how he loved me because he didn't. That man ain't never did nothing for me."

"Now you are lying! I ain't gone let you make a fool out of my brother. He's a good man. He's a preacher." Henry Lee explained.

"Preacher?" I said as a disgusting taste formed in my mouth.

"Pastor." He corrected me while having the audacity to sit his drink on my table. "Sorry to hear about your Mama. She was a good woman."

"He's a molester! He's a fucking child molester. That's what he is. How dare you stand in front of me and talk about that man like he is some type of god. He is a child molester."

"Lower your voice." Henry Lee said.

"I'm not going to be quiet!" I said as my voice quivered. He looked like Richard. He sounded like Richard. "I waited. I waited. I waited over thirty years for this moment." I said realizing that I had indeed waited over thirty years for this moment. I struggled to catch my breath. He turned to walk away.

"I'll burn this whole fuckin' place to the ground! You ain't gonna just walk away from me! You took everything from me." I raged following him. "Don't walk away from me Richard!" I screamed. He turned to me. He almost seemed to have sympathy in his eyes.

"Baby, I'm not Richard. I'm Henry." He said. I felt the room watching me.

"Nette, come on let's go." Stacey said as she wrapped her arm around me. She cried.

"Don't touch me!" I shouted. I grabbed my purse and walked to my car. I do not remember what happened next, but within the next hour I found myself in Craig's bed.

"Seventy. Eighty. Ninety. One hundred." I heard him count. I felt the money fall on my naked breast as I stared into the ceiling fan above me. I didn't collect the money. This time, it was not about the money. I did not care about my bills or anything else. I just needed to feel a distraction from what had just erupted with Henry Lee. I had learned long ago to mentally disconnect with men during sex, so I almost did not even acknowledge Craig was present until he jammed his penis into me. He was brutal, and he was demeaning.

"Ouch." I said.

"Shut the fuck up." He said. "All the niggas you mess with, this ain't hurting you." He said thrusting into me. "Put your legs up." He insisted. I ignored him. How dare Henry Lee refer to Richard as if he was worthy of being called my father. I had a biological father, and I loved him. I *did not* love Richard. I never loved Richard, and he never loved me. "I said put your fucking legs up, hoe." Craig raged, tossing my legs over my head. I felt a pain in my lower back. Still, I said nothing. I was quiet.

Aside from my biological father there was Eric. Eric was the man I believed to be my mother's one true love. He adored her, and he adored me even though their relationship failed. Richard was in no way a father to me and the idea that anyone could award him that title over my life made me angry.

"Shit." Craig said pulling himself out of me. He pulled the broken condom from him and threw it to the floor. He searched his wallet for another condom. Craig returned to the bed. "I don't want to see that." Craig said before throwing me on my stomach. He jumped on top of me. I'm not sure when I began crying, but I cried, and my tears angered him. "Bitch, you better not give me shit either or I swear to god that I'll beat your ass." He jammed himself into me again. He was not passionate or caring with me. He did not love me, and he made deliberate efforts to be certain that I did not confuse what we were doing with making love. "You gone always come get this dick because you know ain't nobody else gonna give you a dime for it."

I felt as if I would hyperventilate. What was happening to me? Why could I hear Craig's hateful words to me? He forced my face into the mattress as I struggled for air. "You gonna always come get this." He repeated. I became angry that I could not escape from this moment as I had done so since I was a little girl beneath Richard. I told myself that I just had to focus more, and that it would be over soon. "Always!" he reiterated. No matter how much I tried, prayed, and longed for it, the escape would never occur again. "Damn, always!"

"I said NO!" I shouted as I elbowed him. "No".

CHAPTER EIGHT

The Truth of My Tears

 Healing is a woman's prerogative. Nothing that I experienced, lived, felt, or grabbed in life told me that I was not healed quite like the moment when the man who robbed me of my childhood stood before me. Over thirty years had passed since I had seen Richard, and in that moment with Henry Lee I realized a much more painful truth. I had not seen myself in almost thirty years either. You see, I left myself in that bed the last time my mother's boyfriend climbed on top of me and put his penis on me.

 I made a decision to escape from the moment of shame, and abuse. I believed that if I could just get my mind to escape what was happening to my body in that moment, that it would soon be over. You see, the human mind is an amazing instrument. It has the ability to pretty much do whatever you need it to do, but it won't do what you want it to do so easily. Well, my mind knew that I needed to escape from my body as I prepared to be assaulted again, so it rewarded me with just that. I left my body that night as Marietta, thirty plus years ago. In that moment Richard was not on top of me. I was not bitter towards my father, and I was a fully grown woman able to provide, care, and protect herself. I was no longer a child. I was a strong woman with a family and a husband who loved her. Oh, the escape was so peaceful and glorious that I could not even feel his thrust between my legs. The tighter I held my eyes closed, the deeper the escape seemed. After a few moments, the sound of my bedroom door shutting ended my escape. My eyes opened. Richard was gone and my blankets were covering me as if nothing had happened. Something had happened, something happened that could not be undone. My eyes opened, but I never went back to being fourteen-year-old Nettie Pooh. I was now Marietta, and while everyone would continue calling me otherwise, I knew that Marietta was not a child. She would not think as a child, lust as a child, behave as a child, or want as a child. She was a grown woman in a child's body, and she had to do what she believed grown women did to feel safe from the dark.

Grandma's baby, Mama's angel, and Uncle Ken's doll was gone. Had I known that my great escape would mean I would enter a world that only I would exist in for the next thirty plus years, then maybe I would have ran from Richard, screamed louder, or taken any other measures to remove myself from him. I lost myself that night and it was only when the now forty plus year old Marietta stared her monster in the eyes that I realized what he took from me.

You see I knew that my mother truly hated Richard for what he did to me, and I forgave her. I knew that she loved me until her last breath, however there was still something missing. For so long I looked to her to give me what was missing, but what was missing was me. Richard took me from me, and he defined who Marietta would be and what she needed to feel whole. I no longer had an authentic version of myself that was able to be the daughter, granddaughter, mother, or wife that those I loved needed me to be. I lived the next few decades as the figment of my imagination that was created in the moment in which I was first assaulted as a child by Richard. Whenever anyone in my life performed, acted, or behaved in a way contrary to the Marietta that existed now, I had to divorce, breakup, run, or even abort them.

All that I had to hold on to was the woman I became when I first escaped from myself, so I spent years trying to fulfill the life this woman had that made me feel safe when I was fourteen years old. In my escape, I gave myself a life that I could love, and from the next morning following the first attack from Richard, I began seeking to build that life that I escaped to so I never had to return to being just his victim, Nettie Pooh. So, I found Quincy. I found Antonio, TJ, David, Andre, Chad, Malcolm, Omar, Juan, Craig, and many more. I found pregnancies after pregnancies, relationships, sex, drugs, prostitution, and alcohol. The woman I escaped into being was not real. She could never be real with herself, her children, her family, and none of the men she slept with or loved along the way.

Many times, over the next thirty years I became angry because no one called me by the name, Nettie Pooh. Sometimes I thought as if I could just hear the name, that I could return to that girl. Instead, they all called me Nette or Jeannette. Well, that angered me, because that was the name of the woman everyone expected to be. Strong, healed, hole, secured, confident, and in control. Dammit I was none of that, and Marietta was drowning trying to swim in Jeannette's ocean. I wasn't as strong, confident, and capable as they all thought. I became angry that I couldn't show them my truth. Then I became angry that no one could see my truth. I felt abandoned. They all assumed that everything I did, I did so because I wanted it. That was not my truth. Marietta did not want all those failed relationships, marriages, and addictions. She wanted the idea of family that kept her safe from the dark. So, I didn't care if I had one husband or one hundred husbands. I was going to keep building and reaching for the things Marietta needed to feel safe.

By the time I had the husbands, houses, children, and cars that I wanted for the life I believed meant that I was safe, I was left still feeling afraid of the dark. The moment that I realized that nothing or no one that I had accumulated over my life, would ever make me feel what the first image of Marietta made me feel, I lost it. When I realized that the vision of Marietta that I had was not reachable, I had nothing to catch me from this fall. I suffered mental breakdown after breakdowns. I became suicidal. I wanted to die because I did not know how to be anyone other than a woman just trying to feel better. I was exhausted, and my life was not my own.

But there I was naked in bed with Craig; another man who did not love me. I wanted to scream, because in that moment I knew that all my roads of shame led back to Richard.

"Get your muthafuckin hands off of me!" Nettie Pooh screamed. Oh, dear God. Nettie Pooh screamed, and I knew that it was her. I exhaled and Marietta died from my soul. With that breath Marietta left and Nettie Pooh returned. She finally screamed. Craig froze. I lowered my head between my legs. I put my hands on my knees. I cried, but it was not pain. God did not have to do it because I did not deserve it. I had not worked for it, but he did it. He gave me back Nettie Pooh. I slowly lifted my head as tears of joy fell from my face to his shoes. I stared him in the eyes. I had never seen such fear. I held his entire life in my hands, and all this time I wanted him to suffer. Now, I saw it. He suffered, and he would continue to suffer. Craig stood near the dresser naked. He looked shocked. I dressed.

"You ain't getting my money. You ain't getting my money. You know you ain't going nowhere. You gonna be right back in my bed." So many times, before I knew that he was right. I knew that many men were right, but this time was different. I knew that when I covered my body and walked away from this house, I would never return. So, I did it. I walked away.

My father was never around in the capacity that I needed him. While Uncle Ken was such a blessing, I needed to know how a man is supposed to love a woman intimately. My father had his own thing going on in life which usually kept him preoccupied with his own chaotic happenings. So, after observing my Mama's relationship with Richard for so long, it had a horrible impact on me. Things would be different, and I knew it from the moment I left Craig standing erect in his bedroom. You see, I did not just leave Craig unsatisfied. In that moment, I left them all standing there.

I knew that I now had the control and right to decide who I wanted to be and what I needed to feel safe. Everything that Richard took from me got it back when I finally stood up to Craig. Richard robbed me of myself, my mother, and my faith. He robbed me of intimacy. I mean, I had six children. Of course, I had sex, but I was incapable of having intimacy. Sex was never intimate, as there was never a moment that sex did not feel like rape even when it was with a man that I loved. I kept telling myself that maybe I didn't love the man at all, and maybe that was the reason for my inability to truly connect. So, I slept with many men, and when I realized that I could not share intimacy with any men whatsoever I lowered my expectations of sex. I lowered my expectations of sex so drastically, that sex even became a business that I used to take care of my children. At times I found myself as a prostitute for men that treated my body as a toy. They would push me, pull me, with no care whatsoever. I would further escape into Marietta just as I learned to do thirty years prior.

I no longer needed or desired to be the emotionless, empty, and troubled Marietta. I walked away from Craig that night almost running and racing to get home to my children, and now, grandchildren. For a moment, I feared that no one would love me now. On my way home that night, I found God in a way that I had never found Him before. I felt free. I no longer felt shame, self-condemnation, regret, and hatred towards myself. I was no longer angry at my father, Antonio or anyone who disappointed me.

Today, I have learned who I am, and to be honest I find myself more and more every day. I'm no longer the little girl Nettie Pooh. I'm no longer the drunken Marietta. I am my own Jeannette, and she has dreams, goals, and desires that have nothing to do with a man. I have dreams of entrepreneurship. I have dreams of teaching, speaking, and healing other women who escaped to places they should have never fled just as I did. I had spent so long trying to reach who I thought I needed to be, that I never sought who I could be. I wish I could say that I am fully healed of all my hurts, but that is not so. Healing is an ongoing process. I still find myself being fully dressed for bed, as I did as a little girl to avoid attacks from Richard. I still find myself fearing the dark. But you know what? I am okay with that because I know that my pain will not last forever. Healing belongs to me, and I embrace and welcome it in whatever fashion it comes. I am not a product of my pain. I am victorious. I have learned that surviving is what I do best, and I wear my ability to persevere as a breastplate of strength. I am a survivor.

    I have learned to be at peace with any tears that I shed today because I know that my soul is no longer suffering. I learned to love myself more graciously with every passing day. I am excited, I am thrilled, and I am confident in my tomorrow. I may not know what tomorrow holds, but God is there. He is here, and He is mine. I escaped into God and the peace of His spirit. He is my savior, my deliverer, and most of all He is mine. And because of that, I cannot lose Him, and I cannot lose me.

THE END

A Letter To my Children

Dear Kings and Queens,

    I watched you live and grow and grieve. I made many mistakes that hurt your growth greatly. However, you did not let that stop you. No matter what, I continued to love you even if I did not say it much. You lacked hugs and kisses because I lacked hugs and kisses from my mother. On your way to breaking generational curses from all of life's downfalls. I have seen you pick yourselves up and dust yourselves off, even when people gave up on you. Even when the world gave up on you.

    My rearing you might not have been the best. But it was all that I knew. If given a chance to start over, I would protect you from all the evils of the world that lurked behind trees and within the clouds while I lay naked and drunk in my own pains. At times feeling like my legs were broken and my breath was no more. I lay down with many; for the money, as my soul was sucked away from my body. Just know there were days that I went without eating so you could. The jobs that I worked, sometimes two at a time to make sure that your needs were met. When I could not afford to buy the food and clothes we needed, I stole them.

    I was so desperately needing to protect you from the closed caskets of your father's everlasting memories and the torment of grief and anguish. For every family member that has disowned you, missed special events in your life, or just missed your growth altogether, using their unhealthy relationships with me as an excuse. I am asking from the depth of my very broken, tired, and dismembered soul to please forgive me for all the aches and pains I have caused throughout your lives. God, my God. I apologize from every piece of my broken heart. Like children in the park throwing sand in each other's hair and mouth. And we all know how hard it is to remove sand.

     Please know that each of you hold an incredibly special place in my life. If not for you I would have ended this pitiful life of mine a long time ago. You make life worth living. I will say today 1 million times forever that I love you. There is nothing more precious than a mother's love for her children.

Now I lay me down to sleep
I pray the Lord my Soul to keep
If I should die before I wake
I pray the Lord my Soul to take
Please do not take life for granted
Today is the day the Lord has made
Rejoice and be glad in it
You are special and unique in every way
Living and obtaining the knowledge each day
To carry you through life and make choices of the wise
The day will come when I have to say my good-byes
And when I do you can look back and say

My mom became a mother, for this we always prayed
Through the pain and struggles I would do it again
My Kings and Queens you are true blessings from beginning to end

Special Thanks

Author, Keaires Roberson,
I Was A Wife Before You Found Me.

Demetrius Malone & McKinley Harris
DemiCo National, LLC

Maleeka Hollaway,
The OMG LLC.

I would further like to give a special thanks to all my friends and family that supported me and helped me along this process. I appreciate your time, prayers, and patience. There were many days I felt like giving up. Staying up late nights crying and praying asking God for peace and inner strength. However, you all continued to push me through. I could not have done this on my own. I love you.

www.ingramcontent.com/pod-product-compliance
Lightning Source LLC
Chambersburg PA
CBHW071008080526
44587CB00015B/2392